# LINE TO THE
# STARS

## SIXTY YEARS OF FILMING AT
## THE BLUEBELL RAILWAY

HEIDI MOWFORTH

AMBERLEY

*Front cover*: top: Stephen Fry and Hugh Laurie as Jeeves and Wooster; clockwise from top: Michelle Dockery, Dan Stevens and Laura Carmichael at Downton station; David Suchet as Hercule Poirot; Jeremy Brett and Edward Hardwicke as Holmes and Watson (Granada TV); Jenny Agutter as Mother in *The Railway Children* (Carlton TV).

*Back cover*: Ralph Fiennes, director and playing the role of Charles Dickens in *The Invisible Woman*.

All other photos are by Mick Blackburn or from the Bluebell Railway Archive.

First published 2024

Amberley Publishing
The Hill, Stroud,
Gloucestershire, GL5 4EP

www.amberley-books.com

ISBN: 978 1 3981 2030 3 (print)
ISBN: 978 1 3981 2031 0 (ebook)

British Library Cataloguing in Publication Data.
A catalogue record for this book is available from the British Library.

Typeset in 10pt on 13pt Celeste.
Typesetting by SJmagic DESIGN SERVICES, India.
Printed in the UK.

# Contents

# Introduction

For more than 150 years, railways have held a special place in the hearts and minds of the British people. Railway stations, railway lines, tunnels and the trains themselves have been appropriate settings for romance, comedy, drama and the supernatural in literature and film from the earliest days of the iron road; indeed, the earliest surviving moving picture was of a train arriving at a station, which was said to have terrified audiences to whom it was first shown.

Railway stations have been the scene of many an emotionally charged meeting and parting, from the famous 'Oh my daddy, my daddy' scene at the end of *The Railway Children* to scenes of young soldiers leaving for the front in two world wars, never to return again to England. One of the most famous romances of all time, *Brief Encounter*, was set in the seemingly humdrum surroundings of Carnforth station buffet, and the scenes there have been repeated in pastiche countless times, many of them at the Bluebell Railway. Drama and danger also made the most of railway background from the earliest days; the silent films of the 1920s include many heart-stopping railway stunts, and Buster Keaton was no stranger to hair-raising adventures on the iron road, in the days when it was no big deal to have an entire train fall into a river in the cause of celluloid entertainment.

In sixty-plus years at the Bluebell, we have seen it all. We have travelled the world, visited numerous different stations, both real and fictional, met a wide variety of characters and had many adventures along the way. This book explores that journey from the first film made at the railway in 1960 to some of the most recent.

One wonders what film makers would have done without the emergence of the heritage railway movement, which began with the little locomotive *Stepney* at the Bluebell in 1960 and now covers Britain in a network of volunteer-run railways. Suppose that those few pioneers in the early days had failed in their efforts to buy and preserve Sheffield Park station, the railway line and those first engines and carriages. Presumably railway scenes would have been portrayed somehow – using archive footage, models, and, in later years, computer graphics – but the disappearance of steam, vintage carriages and original stations would have been as much of a loss to the film industry as to our heritage.

*Heidi Mowforth*

# 1

# The 1960s

## A New Film Location is Born

During the early 1960s the Bluebell Railway in East Sussex was just getting established, both as the UK's first standard-gauge railway to be privately run by volunteers, as a tourist attraction and as a film location.

In those early days, the railway, with its headquarters based at Sheffield Park station on the main Lewes to East Grinstead road, didn't even run as far as Horsted Keynes, 5 miles distant, so our most used location, Horsted Keynes station, wasn't open for business. It was still at the end of an electrified branch line from Haywards Heath until 1963 and Bluebell trains stopped just short of the station at Bluebell Halt – a makeshift platform next to the road. Steam-hauled trains on the Southern didn't finish until 1967 and in order to film a steam train in those days, it wasn't, of course, necessary to go to a heritage railway, and filming techniques were far less sophisticated than they are now. Studio shots of train interiors were often cut in with archive shots of trains on the line, and fewer pains were taken with set dressing and the authenticity of props than they are now. The Bluebell came into its own when a particular period look was required or when the scene couldn't be easily filmed at any other railway location and the film crews could be certain of having a stretch of line to themselves.

Our first ever 'film job' was *The Innocents* in 1961, followed by adverts for Rowntree's Fruit Gums, Burton's tailoring and Microsel (whatever that was).

*Anna Karenina* and *Waltz of the Toreadors* followed in 1961, with *Khartoum* and *I'll Never Forget What's 'isname* later in that decade.

## The Innocents

This film, by producer Jack Clayton, was based on the Victorian ghost story by Henry James, *The Turn of the Screw*. Governess Miss Giddens takes a job looking after two orphaned children under the care of their uncle, who has to leave the country for an unspecified length of time. They reside in a large Gothic mansion with the housekeeper,

Mrs Grose. The children were previously under the care of a tutor, Mr Quint, and a governess, Miss Jessel, who seem to have had an inappropriate relationship, both dying in dubious and mysterious circumstances. They continue to haunt the house – or do they? Is it all a product of Miss Giddens' imagination or do the children really see things and say nothing? The implied ghosts in the book are sinister enough, but in the film it's the children who are really creepy.

The boy, Miles, is sent home from boarding school for 'corrupting' his school chums, although how he does is never explained, either in the book or the film. Miss Giddens and Miles' sister, Flora, go to meet him at the station, which is set at Sheffield Park. The house and gardens on the nearby Sheffield Park estate were used for the exteriors of the haunted house, so the station was convenient in more ways than one. Miles arrives in the Metropolitan carriage set, hauled by loco No. 55 *Stepney*, to greet his sister and governess on the platform.

The Bluebell's first ever filming contract, *The Innocents*, in 1961, starred Deborah Kerr, seen here plugging her ears as the safety valve lifts on No. 323 *Bluebell*.

## Anna Karenina

A BBC production, based on the epic novel written by Tolstoy. The drama and tragedy culminate in the final scene, when Anna tells her faithful maid that she is 'going to catch a train' and rushes out to the station in the snow. Far from catching a train, she walks in front of it, ending her life and the story.

Sheffield Park was adorned with fake snow (the filming took place in June) and *Stepney* was given a large smokestack-style chimney to represent a Russian engine.

A camera was placed in the locomotive maintenance pit in order to film the underside and wheels of the carriages as they hurtled over the tragic heroine, at no little danger to the cameraman, who, in those days, had to be present in the pit with his camera. Claire Bloom, who played Anna, was filmed coming out onto the platform and then the scene was cut to the rushing wheels before the final credits.

Two television programmes were then filmed at Sheffield Park; ITV filmed part of an episode of *No Hiding Place* entitled 'Signals at Danger' and the BBC filmed part of *The Vanishing Steam Engine* (steam traction was to finally end on the national network in 1968 and the writing was already on the wall).

Loco No. 55 *Stepney* was given a simple Russian makeover with the addition of a further number and a giant smokestack for the filming of Tolstoy's *Anna Karenina* in 1961.

## Waltz of the Toreadors

Unlike the first two films made at the railway, this one was in glorious colour. Based on the play by Jean Anouilh, it was billed as a 'saucy sex romp' (or what passed for one in 1961) about a retired military officer, played by Peter Sellers, unable to keep his eyes off the girls. The film unit was at the railway for four days, on the lineside and at the station, filming two scenes. The first necessitated the building of a flimsy and very makeshift level crossing at a farm crossing near Three Arch Bridge. There the wronged wife sits on the crossing in a suicide attempt – just after the train had passed. The second scene, at Sheffield Park, involved a rather daring stunt with the hero riding a horse at some speed after the departing train, along the lineside. In a studio shot, he pulls the heroine out of the train and rides off with her. The train used was the Metropolitan Railway carriage set, in the brown-painted livery that it only carried for the duration of 1961, and therefore the only time that the set appeared on film in that colour.

All this activity in 1961 had put the Bluebell firmly on the map as far as film work was concerned and more jobs followed later in the decade.

In 1965 Sherlock Holmes and Dr Watson made their first visit to the line, to film scenes for *The Retired Colourman*. Engine No. 473 *Birch Grove* hauled the train on that occasion.

In 1966 big names Charlton Heston and Laurence Olivier came to film scenes for their epic *Khartoum*. The British prime minister of 1883 was played by Ralph Richardson; General Charles Gordon by Charlton Heston; and the Muslim fanatic, the Mahdi, by Laurence Olivier.

The wronged wife sits on a makeshift level crossing in a suicide attempt in *Waltz of the Toreadors*.

The BBC came to film shots for *The Forsyte Saga* in 1966 and Thames TV were not to feel left out with their visit in connection with the TV series about the fictional detective Sexton Blake.

The railway-based scenes required for the 1966 comedy film *The Wrong Box*, based on Robert Louis Stephenson's 1889 novel, were undertaken on the line.

## *I'll Never Forget What's 'isname*

By 1967 the Bluebell was running into Horsted Keynes station, but the rather ramshackle previous 'northern outpost' of Bluebell Halt was still in situ. Producer and director Michael Winner was making a film about an advertising agency, and the scene at the Bluebell was of the ad men characters filming an advert featuring a ghost train.

Bluebell Halt was transformed with a station building setup, all painted white. Orson Welles played lusty tycoon advertising executive Jonathan Lute in charge of making the advert, and Oliver Reed, as Andrew Quint, his disillusioned TV-ad genius employee, engaged in a dalliance with his leading lady Lyn Ashley (Susannah) when he ought to have been concentrating on making the advert.

The North London Railway tank locomotive and a set of carriages were painted white for the filming to match the white ghost station. The film was quite controversial at the time and is often named as the first mainstream film to use the F-word.

Naturally there's a lady tied to the track for *I'll Never Forget What's 'isname.*

# 2

# The 1970s

## The Start of a Filming Boom

With the closure of the electrified branch in 1963 by British Railways and the subsequent purchase by Bluebell of Horsted Keynes station, it wasn't long before it began to come into its own as a film location for a wide variety of different settings. There were several important points in its favour: many film crews were based in London, and Horsted Keynes isn't too far away and has ample private parking suitable for large film units. It is also in a conveniently out of the way spot, away from the gaze of interested members of the public and unwanted press attention.

Volunteers at the Bluebell were swift to realise that accommodating film crews paid dividends. Apart from the actual filming fees (which, in the 1970s, were probably very underpriced) there was the publicity, particularly on prime-time television and the 1970s were the beginning of a filming boom. Advertising stills, TV adverts, documentaries, children's programmes, serials and cinema films – some with an obvious railway theme, others with very tenuous links – all came to film at the Bluebell, mainly at Horsted Keynes.

A strong chocolate biscuit theme seemed to be running through TV advertising at the time; all three TV channels put in an appearance and Ken Russell was the most prominent film director of the decade to make good use of the location.

## Advertising: The Chocolate-Biscuit Years

The Bluebell soon became the backdrop for advertising a wide variety of products. There were plenty of TV adverts for the latest products and a few government agencies of the time, such as the Gas Council and the Egg Marketing Board, which had the engine crew frying numerous eggs on a specially polished shovel on the GWR Dukedog engine in an attempt to persuade the nation to 'go to work on an egg'.

Some of the adverts mirrored products of the age, while others are still available today. Vicks Lozenges, Sirdar Wools and Dewar's Whisky are still around, but Ever Ready batteries have been superseded, at least in the advertising stakes, by the Duracell 'Bunny'.

Sadly, Viyella nylon shirts are no longer the epitome of cool and although Babycham has been rebranded and repackaged, I don't know what a twenty-first-century bartender would say to a request for it, but all these, among others, were advertised with the Bluebell as a backdrop.

In November 1975 Yardley lipstick went to town at Horsted Keynes, turning it into Kapenh, supposedly in Russia, with the Adams Radial Tank No. 488 made up as a Russian engine. Fake snow adorned the platform, which was meant to be biodegradable but hung around on the hedges for months.

In 1977, the lineside was used to excellent advantage to advertise Winalot dog biscuits. A train hauled by C Class locomotive No. 592 passed by, complete with the picturesque plume of white smoke and steam from the chimney, and in the foreground a 1920s couple enjoyed a picnic in the field by the side of their 1926 Austin Chummy and frolicked with a brown spaniel. This was a typical case of the railway not having to do much – just lay on a passing train as a backdrop as the voiceover starts: 'Winalot – as good today as it's always been.'

Immac hair remover had a tall, glamorous model walking onto the platform and climbing onto the footplate of the standard tank No. 80064, from where she proceeded

Now we are in colour and the ubiquitous 'girl tied to the track' returned in 1972 for Dewar's Whisky.

A horse-drawn sleigh and fake snow get set for the arrival of the train for Yardley's lipstick in November 1975.

to drive it away, and Royal Mail tried to persuade its customers to read postal timetables before posting letters by having comic actor Bob Todd chasing engine No. 263 down the line on a pump trolley – 'should have read the timetable'.

In 1970, it took four days to dress Horsted Keynes station to make an advert for Toffee Crisp. The station was turned into the stage of a lavish musical, peopled by dancers in garish costumes who tripped their way along the platform and descended from the train in synchronisation as they encouraged us to 'chew chew a toffee crisp' (see what they did there?).

Cilla Black made a series of memorable adverts for Cadbury's Dairy Milk, marketed as 'chunky' with 'a glass and a half of full-cream milk in every half pound' back in the day when dairy wasn't scary. Cilla spent two days at Horsted Keynes in January 1978, gallivanting around the station stuffing squares of chunky Dairy Milk into the mouths of unsuspecting station staff and passengers alighting from a train hauled by engine No. 30064.

In October 1978 Bill Oddie and Derek Guyler made an advert for Bandit biscuits, with Guyler as the ticket inspector and Oddie the bandit. Oddie arrives at Horsted Keynes with a large amount of luggage then presents a Bandit biscuit instead of a valid ticket. Ticket Inspector Guyler calculates that a ticket from Mexico to Horsted Keynes would be about

*Above left*: Comic actor Bob Todd chases the train on a pump trolley for a Royal Mail advert in May 1978.

*Above right*: Cilla Black extols the virtues of 'chunky' Cadbury's Dairy Milk chocolate.

£3,000 and Oddie draws a gun and says that he will have to rob a bank for that sort of money. 'Bandit – the most wanted biscuit in Britain.'

In 1977 Horsted Keynes station was the setting for one of the most clever and amusing adverts of the chocolate-biscuit period – Taxi biscuits. A custom-built bright-blue taxi was constructed on the chassis of a Robin Reliant and given eccentric wheels so that it bounced along when in motion. It appeared in the station drive, and the driver presented the ticket inspector with a Taxi biscuit at the side gate to the platform before it drove onto the station. It proceeded along the platforms, showering biscuits from a compressed-air-operated biscuit dispenser in the cab.

Even more hair-raising stunts were performed in March 1979 by a Spanish film crew advertising Lois jeans, an advert unfortunately never shown in the UK. The stuntman, clad in Lois jeans, jumped from a galloping horse onto a moving train, off a bridge onto the roof of a train, and rode a motorcycle up a ramp and into a wagon on the rear of a passing train.

*Left*: Bill Oddie, dressed as a Mexican, with ticket collector Derek Guyler for Bandit biscuits, October 1977.

*Below*: A custom-built bright-blue taxi was made for a Taxi biscuits commercial, which included travelling down the subway steps after the film crew's carpenters had removed the handrails and built a wooden floor over the steps.

# 3

# The Ken Russell Period

Ken Russell (1927–2011) was one of the most controversial film directors of the 1960s, 1970s and 1980s. His pioneering films were often based – some of them rather loosely – on the lives of composers and artists; some famous and some not.

Attracting criticism for being obsessed with sexuality and the Church, all his films were made in his own avant-garde, flamboyant style, and he always showed a great interest in that line in the human psyche where genius and madness are inclined to meet.

Four of his most celebrated films had the Bluebell as a background and featured Bluebell volunteers as extras.

## *Savage Messiah* (1972)

This film told the story of the obscure French sculptor Henri Gaudier Brzeska and his complicated platonic relationship with the Polish novelist Sophie Brzeska, whose name he chose to add to his own. Sophie was twice Henri's age when he met her, aged eighteen, but the relationship was sadly short-lived; he died in the trenches, fighting for France, in 1915. He was twenty-three.

Henri was played by Scott Anthony and Sophie by Dorothy Tutin, and both were at the railway for two days' filming. Three engines were required, all hauling trains through the station to give the appearance of a busy Portland station.

In a closely choreographed scene, Henri arrives on Platform 2 on the local train as the 'express' arrives at Platforms 4/5. Both trains depart again, and Henri, his arms full of daffodils, catches sight of Sophie on Platform 5. Anxious to reach her, and, with the impetuosity of youth, reluctant to go the long way round, he jumps down onto the timber foot crossing. As he is about to climb up onto Sophie's platform, he drops his handful of daffodils and scrabbles around trying to pick them all up as No. 30064 bears rapidly down upon him with a rake of loose-coupled wagons. Henri manages to scramble up on the platform edge at the last minute with his arms full of battered daffodils for Sophie.

Director Ken Russell (left) turns the handle to check the camera angle on the foot crossing at Horsted Keynes for *Savage Messiah*.

## *Mahler* (1974)

This film explores the life of composer Gustav Mahler, viewed through a series of flashbacks from the vantage point of one long train journey. Towards the end of his life, Mahler (Robert Powell) travels from Bavaria to Vienna with his wife (Georgina Hale). This is a time of mutual self-discovery for the couple, and the flashback sequences depict scenes from Mahler's traumatic past. His dysfunctional family life, the suicide of his brother, his conversion from

Filming *Mahler* at Horsted Keynes with Bluebell volunteer extras in October 1973.

Judaism to Catholicism, and the deaths of his young children are all explored in graphic and uncompromising detail to a background of the composer's stirring music.

Filming the train journey that forms the backbone of the film took eight days during October 1973. Standard 4 engine No. 75027 hauled the train repeatedly between Sheffield Park and Horsted Keynes, which became four different stations in Germany and Austria.

## *Tommy* (1975)

A film version of The Who's 1969 rock opera, boasting a cast list packed with names from the pop scene of the day. Roger Daltrey, Ann Margret, Oliver Reed, Elton John, Tina Turner, Jack Nicholson, Paul Nicholas and The Who all appeared in the film, which spent fourteen weeks at No. 1 in the film charts and played to full houses for over a year.

Tommy Walker is a boy struck deaf and blind by a childhood trauma who becomes a master pinball player and religious cult figure. Through the extravagance of music and drama he encounters such bizarre and colourful characters as the Pinball Wizard and the Acid Queen – as unashamedly over the top as the rest of the film.

Filming at the Bluebell only took one day in June 1974, and most of the shots featured loco No. 75027 with its train at night. It left Horsted Keynes in the direction of East Grinstead, heavily enhanced by electric headlamps and an electric glow from the firebox.

The honeymoon of RAF Group Captain Walker (Robert Powell) and his wife Nora (Ann Margret) at the railway for *Tommy* in June 1974.

## *Lisztomania* (1975)

'The film that out-Tommys Tommy' topped the box office for two weeks and starred Roger Daltrey (as Franz Liszt), Paul Nicholas, Ringo Starr, Rick Wakeman, Sara Kestelman and Fiona Lewis.

The film explores the relationship between Liszt and Wagner, and the claim that many of Wagner's musical ideas had been 'stolen' from Liszt. It was described by one critic as 'A berserk exercise of demented genius'. Words used to describe the film include 'electrifying, erotic, exotic' and it is billed as 'a film of prodigious imagination'.

In May 1975, some of this prodigious imagination went into the filming of a scene involving No. 75 *Fenchurch* and an exploding grand piano. A countess and a pianist are discovered in bed together by the count, who exacts a terrible revenge. He orders his servants to place the lovers inside a grand piano, take it to the station, and leave it on the railway line to allow the passage of trains to finish the job. Two pianos were constructed of balsa wood and primed with explosives and *Fenchurch* and its train were driven at line speed through each one in two separate takes.

*Fenchurch* bears down on the grand piano ...

... which is primed with explosives.

# 4

# The 1970s: Television

## Documentaries

The Bluebell played its part in telling the stories of Rolls-Royce, Suttons Seeds, the suffragettes and the miners' strike of 1844.

In 1973 John Betjeman's *Metro-Land* was filmed on a very wet and slippery June day, with P Class No. 27 hauling the Metropolitan Railway coaches. Betjeman is filmed inside the refreshment room at Horsted Keynes prior to boarding the coaches.

Poet Laureate John Betjeman exits the refreshment room at Horsted Keynes to board his train for *Metroland*.

# Children's Programmes

In December 1971, the disused Bluebell Halt was once again pressed back into service, this time to represent a station in Canada for a BBC adaptation of *Anne of Green Gables*. A waiting room was built and palisade fencing and false trees were added, the scene being filmed from a passing platelayers' trolley.

A disused railway station was required for the comedy children's show *Funny Ha Ha* on Thames TV. Sheffield Park stood in as the station and a goods van acquired a new livery of yellow with purple spots.

One of the most popular 1970s children's programmes was *Crackerjack*. 'It's Friday, it's five to five. It's Crackerjack!' With its mix of audience participation, silly games and daft jokes, every episode included a short silent film, featuring presenters Peter Glaze and Don Maclean taking on a variety of jobs to which they were singularly unsuited: window cleaner, road sweeper, stable hand, etc. They tried their hand at becoming railwaymen and came to Sheffield Park to spend a chaotic time on the train and the footplate. A stuntman fell from the footplate of the engine over the bridge and into the river, but it was Maclean who appeared in the water. Somehow, Don Maclean always seemed to end up in the drink.

BBC *Crackerjack's* Peter Glaze and Don Maclean try their hand at being railwaymen in February 1973.

## Tommy Steele in Search of Charlie Chaplin

In 1971 a BBC film crew spent two days at Horsted Keynes, filming *Tommy Steele in Search of Charlie Chaplin*, which was transmitted on Easter Monday that year. Tommy Steele sang a music hall song in the Caledonian Railway coach, surrounded by other actors consuming generous quantities of genuine champagne, in an 'interior train' scene that required vast amounts of power. Two generators, one petrol and one diesel, were necessary to power the spotlights, and these were housed in the brake van. These were the days before tight regulations concerning noxious fumes, and guard for the day, Alan Cobden, complained at length about the toxic atmosphere in the brakevan, stating that he had a sore throat for several days afterwards.

## Features

In 1972 Horsted Keynes was the scene for two of the most popular shows of the day. The BBC turned up with *Englebert Humperdinck with the Young Generation*, when Horsted Keynes became 'Generation Gap' for the day. Englebert and the Young Generation performed a song from their new album. Englebert was on the footplate of No. 323 *Bluebell* clad in overalls and a greasetop hat, while the Young Generation danced energetically on the running plate of the engine and along the platform.

Thames TV brought along American singing star Tony Bennett, star of *Talk of the Town*, to hurtle through a day in the life of the railway, playing the part of ticket collector, porter, signalman ... you name it. In 1973 well-known radio and television comedy double act Elsie and Doris Waters visited Horsted Keynes to make the film *Wish You Were Here*, featuring a Victorian special excursion to Brighton hauled by No. 72 *Fenchurch*.

Englebert Humperdinck suitably clad in engine overalls and hat.

# TV Serials

In the 1920s and 1930s, a group of women crime writers became part of what was known as the golden age of detective fiction. Among these was Dorothy L. Sayers, who, in her literary style, wrote several that involved murders with intricate and complicated plots, solved in the end by her detective, Lord Peter Wimsey, and his 'man', Bunter. Actor Ian Carmichael made the part of Lord Peter his own, both on radio and television. In November 1973 he was at the Bluebell travelling to Southampton (Sheffield Park to Horsted Keynes) aboard a train hauled by the Dukedog. *The Unpleasantness at the Bellona Club* presents Lord Peter with a corpse in an exclusive gentleman's club. Not an unusual occurrence, you may think, but it comes close enough upon the death of the gentleman's only estranged sister to raise all sorts of questions as to who actually died first, who inherits, and was he pushed? The journey to Southampton so that Lord Peter could interview relatives was made more interesting on that November day by damp, fog and a certain amount of engine-slipping up Freshfield Bank.

*Colditz* was one of the most popular serials of the 1970s, set inside the notorious Colditz Castle, the most impregnable prison that the Germans had for intractable British prisoners, particularly those who had managed to escape from other prisons. This stronghold was the ultimate challenge for British escapees, and the series entertained the viewer with some of the most ingenious escape plans known to man. In October 1973 a group of British prisoners and their German escorts were conveyed to their new home by the P Class No. 27 and a short goods train. Volunteer Alf Brown's goods van was specially selected for this purpose, as it had the sliding doors typical of many continental vans. The scenes were filmed in daylight, but later made to look as though the journey took place at night.

The 1978 serial *Edward & Mrs Simpson* depicted the developing affair between Edward VIII and the American divorcee Mrs Wallis Simpson, which ultimately led to his abdication so that

Cynthia Harris (Wallace Simpson) and Edward Fox (Edward VIII) at Ballater station.

he could marry her, all other options having been exhausted. Edward Fox played the king, and Cynthia Harris was Wallis Simpson, and it was she who came to Horsted Keynes for a day to catch a train to Ballater, made up of the Bulleid coach set and hauled by H Class No. 263.

One of the iconic comedy series that remains in the national psyche was *On the Buses*. Driver Stan Butler and his clippie and mate Jack Harper, based at the Luxton & District bus depot, were forever getting into scrapes while driving their double-decker to and from the Cemetery Gates and always at odds with Inspector Blake.

In *On the Omnibuses*, 'Blakey' (Stephen Lewis) organises an event at the depot to commemorate the centenary of Luxton & District Buses, with the first motorised bus that the company ever owned on display out in the yard. Stan (Reg Varney) climbs into the cab to see what it was like, and falls asleep, sinking into a dream about driving the bus at the turn of the century. He finds himself taken off the horse-drawn omnibus to which he is accustomed, and made to learn to drive the new horseless bus, with Jack (Bob Grant) as his clippie and Blakey on board. These scenes were filmed along the lanes around Horsted Keynes station, and the bus can clearly be seen approaching the low bridge, Sloop Bridge, as a train passes over it, hauled by the P Class No. 27. The omnibus makes it under the bridge – just. Not so Blakey, who was standing upstairs, facing the wrong way, and ends up hanging onto the girder by his fingertips as Stan explains to Jack that he doesn't know how to reverse the bus in order to go back and get him down. Blakey decides to climb up over the bridge parapet, and is just astride it when another train hurtles past, drain cocks open, scaring him back over the parapet to be left dangling by his fingertips once again. The train was, in fact, the same train, passing in the same direction as the one that had gone by just minutes earlier. Not the first, or the last, time that authenticity has been sacrificed for comic effect. Stephen Lewis did his own stunts for these scenes and was helped down afterwards to mattresses by a handful of Bluebell volunteers who were on the spot.

Stephen Lewis (Inspector Blake) is left dangling from the bridge in *On the Omnibuses*, filmed in January 1973.

# 5

# The 1970s: Films

## Classics of Literature

The subject matter of the films set on the Bluebell during the 1970s varied widely from the classics of literature to dubious pornography.

In 1976 *Men Only* favourite Fiona Richmond made a soft-porn film, *Frankly Fiona,* in which she went through a series of sexual encounters. One of them portrays her being picked up on the lineside by a train hauled by USA tank locomotive No. 30064, following which she and the driver entertain themselves in a way unlikely to promote safe railway operation.

At the other end of the spectrum, adaptations were made of novels by such respectable authors as Bram Stoker and Thomas Hardy. In November 1979, Sheffield Park became one of

Glamour model and actress Fiona Richmond made a soft porn film at the railway in 1976, entitled *Frankly Fiona.*

several stations to pass itself off as Whitby, for the arrival of Count Dracula by night. Unusually, the weather acted up and played its part, and it was a dark, wet, stormy night as the train, hauled by the C Class No. 592 and labelled 'Eastern Yorkshire Railway' pulled in to Platform 1. Two of the biggest acting names of the day, Sir Laurence Olivier and Donald Pleasance, met on the platform amid a blustery swirl of real and fake steam and the glare of the arc lights.

## Tess of the d'Urbervilles

Later that month, the Metropolitan set of coaches appeared in an adaptation of *Tess of the d'Urbervilles*. When the location team came to look around, the set was under restoration in the carriage shed, and the film company offered to fund the rest of the restoration project on the proviso that it would take priority. The task was duly completed, and Horsted Keynes became Sandbourne for the scenes filmed there. The H Class loco No. 263 also took the train for a spin down Freshfield Bank for some passing and interior shots, but these scenes were the only ones filmed in this country. Although the book was set in Dorset, this version was filmed entirely in Brittany.

## Ike: The War Years

In May 1978, both Sheffield Park and Horsted Keynes were used as settings for *Ike: The War Years*, the story of Eisenhower during this time. The Dukedog No. 3217 *Earl of Berkeley* hauled a troop train of four Southern Railway corridor coaches into Horsted Keynes, where a poignant farewell scene was played out. Eisenhower's driver in England, Kay Summersby (played by Lee Renwick), was seeing off her fiancé, an American major, who was subsequently killed in a minefield. After that, Miss Summersby devoted her working life to Eisenhower, and became a Five Star military aide, the first woman in US history to do so.

The scene at Sheffield Park was more complicated to set up, not least because the script required snow, and it was filmed at the end of May. In a liberal sprinkling of condiments, salt was sprinkled on the track, icing sugar on the coaches and foam in the trees. Sheffield Park became Hassalt on the Belgian-German border and the LB&SCR Directors' Saloon became Eisenhower's travelling map room. This was the scene of a meeting between him and Montgomery, which had the potential to alter the course of the war. Eisenhower was played by Robert Duvall and Monty by Ian Richardson, and the film was shown on both British and American TV.

## Adolf Hitler: My Part in His Downfall

The first volume of Spike Milligan's wartime memoirs, covering his training period in the army, was made into a film in 1973. Milligan, played by Jim Dale, joins the 56th Heavy Regiment, Royal Artillery, and the film takes us through a series of madcap adventures and sobering experiences until the day that training is complete, and the 56th are off to war.

Horsted Keynes station, not unfamiliar with scenes of soldiers going off to war, is the stage for the final scenes in the film. They gather on Platform 2 awaiting the train, all laughing and joking together in a tightly packed crowd. The three-coach train, hauled by GWR No. 9017 *Earl of Berkeley*, draws in and the soldiers all pile on board in a noisy rabble.

'Next stop – war!' comments Milligan as the train pulls out, all the men waving caps out of the window as it departs.

Troops gather at Horsted Keynes in September 1972 for Spike Milligan's *Adolf Hitler – My Part in his Downfall*.

6

# The 1980s: Feature Films

## Adventuring and Swashbuckling

By the 1980s, the Bluebell Railway was making quite a name for itself as a filming location, and found its way into a number of films. There was a certain amount of adventuring and swashbuckling going on, and a trend for adaptations of classic works of literature by authors such as Martin Amis and Evelyn Waugh.

Merchant Ivory made a series of films based on the novels of E. M. Forster, which required the most picturesque of Edwardian backdrops – cue Horsted Keynes station.

*Night Train to Murder* was a comedy film made for television by Thames TV, starring comedy duo Eric Morecambe and Ernie Wise alongside Fulton McKay (of *Porridge* fame), which was filmed during a bitterly cold February night in 1983, using the Standard Class No. 75027, which was renumbered 5027 for the night. It was the last piece that Morecambe and Wise worked on together before Eric's death in 1984, Morecambe being in poor health at the time of the filming. It was written as a pastiche of the works of various writers including Agatha Christie and Edgar Wallace, and is set in 1946, featuring Morecambe and Wise ostensibly as 1940s versions of themselves.

Morecambe and Wise at Sheffield Park station for *Night Train to Murder* in 1983.

*The Rules of Comedy* was made in 1987 by an independent film company, and told the story of the coming of the 'talkies' in the late 1920s. Horsted Keynes booking hall and the interior of coach No. 6686 represented, not entirely convincingly, the journey between New York and Hollywood.

It's not often that the Bluebell is called upon to appear more modern than it actually is, but one occasion upon which it did this occurred in 1988 during filming of Martin Amis' first novel *The Rachel Papers*, when the interior of the buffet car had to be dragged reluctantly into the 1960s. This was done largely by covering the brass plates in the bar with a poster advising the traveller to 'Take a Train to Twickenham'.

Later in the same year, Horsted Keynes set the scene for the time of the Boer War, with the North London tank No. 2650 and a three-coach train, crammed with soldiers bidding fond farewells to their loved ones and declaring, in song, what a long way it was to Tipperary. The film, *That Englishwoman*, was directed by a South African gentleman making his last film in England before retiring back home. It was shown only in South Africa, which was a severe disappointment for all the Bluebell volunteers who appeared as extras and never saw the result of their efforts. *Bluebell News* editor Colin Tyson recalls that wardrobe looked him up and down and decided that he'd be the train guard, which, had he known, he would have brought his own better-fitting uniform with him that day.

The novels of E. M. Forster captured an England pre-First World War that was to disappear forever within just a few years. With its strict social codes and rigid class

Your author, Heidi Mowforth, and son Henry (two and a half) in *Emily that Englishwoman*.

system, set against a background of country houses (almost always in summer) and the dreaming spires of university cities, it conjured up a golden time in our history. Merchant Ivory transferred this zeitgeist admirably to the big screen in the 1980s with adaptations of some of these novels, making a series of sumptuous films in delectable locations, backed up by formidable casting and screenplay and attention to detail.

## A Room with a View

Young Lucy Honeychurch (Helena Bonham Carter), as part of her education as a young lady, goes to Florence with a chaperone, her older relative Charlotte Bartlett (Maggie Smith). There she meets George Emerson (Julian Sands) and they have a brief and passionate 'holiday fling'. Back in England, with the passions of Italy presumed behind her, Lucy becomes engaged to the eminently eligible cold fish Mr Vyse. The Italian affair is a thing of the past, until George and his father come to live in the same village as the Honeychurches.

When Charlotte's boiler breaks down she is invited to stay with the Honeychurch family, and arrives at the station (Horsted Keynes, of course) in a train hauled by LBSCR 'Terrier' *Fenchurch*. Fussing with her luggage, she arrives at the ticket booth to be told: 'This ticket is for Dorking – that was the last station.'

'Oh how vexing! I shall have to get a cab.' Just then she is all but bowled over by a young man on a bike, emerging from the underpass and hurtling up the steps – George Emerson, whom she immediately recognises from Florence. She demands to know what he is doing there, and he explains that his father lives there, and he is visiting him. Charlotte is evidently extremely discomfited. Still, she takes the station trap to the Honeychurch residence, seated facing away from the driver. George follows on his bicycle, larking around all the way, Charlotte pointedly ignoring him.

## Maurice

This film, made in 1986, was an adaptation of an E. M. Forster novel exploring the thorny issue of homosexuality in pre-First World War England. Clive Durham (Hugh Grant) and Maurice Hall (James Wilby) meet and fall in love at Cambridge in 1909. Their brief affair (chaste by modern standards) has to be kept secret – any whiff of homosexuality would be reported to the dean or the police. Maurice is eventually sent down by the dean for cutting lectures, seminars, and 'Hall', because he has been gallivanting around in a motorbike and sidecar with Clive for secret trysts in the countryside.

Maurice catches the train home from Cambridge station – the first of many occasions on which Horsted Keynes has played this role. The station is quiet on this particular day; only Clive is on the platform to say goodbye to his friend. As he stands by the train he asks Maurice what he will do – go into his father's firm, is the reply.

'I don't need one of their poxy degrees!'

As the train pulls out, Clive invites Maurice to come and stay at the family seat, Pendersleigh. Once he has graduated, Clive is keen to put his past behind him, becomes the local MP and makes an advantageous marriage, approved by the family. Maurice, however, having failed to 'cure' his homosexuality with hypnotherapy, offends not only sexual sensibilities but social ones by falling in love with Clive's under gamekeeper Alec Scudder (Rupert Graves). Alec goes up to London to meet Maurice at his office, catching the train from his unspecified local station (also Horsted Keynes). A scene was filmed of him buying a ticket and going to wait on an empty platform, merely as a scene to explain Alec's presence in London in his Sunday suit.

## The Dirty Dozen: Next Mission

In 1944 American intelligence gets wind of a proposed assassination attempt on Hitler. Their renowned late entry into the war (again) notwithstanding, the Americans were keen that this shouldn't happen. If the plan succeeded and Hitler was taken out by one of his own generals, there would be a real danger that the German army may become efficient enough to win the war. This had to be prevented, whatever the cost. What was required was for someone expendable to go into Germany, attack the general's train, and kill him before he could get to the Führer. Whether or not they got out again was of little consequence.

Enter Major Reisman (Lee Marvin), a malefactor from the American army with a division of twelve unsavoury characters gathered from a military gaol, most of who were condemned to death. They are billeted at a railway station in England (Horsted Keynes in 1984) to undergo the training necessary to hold up a train. The train provided was a mixed train hauled by the Q Class No. 541. In the first shot of the train, the major is leaning against the cab of the engine to instruct the troops, with fireman Ted Oades looking out over the side in the company of a bulldog. The major explains how to climb up onto the top of a moving carriage and pass along the train on the outside.

'What if they see us, sir?'

'You die.'

'What if we fall off, sir?'

'You die.'

Further training took place by Leamland Bridge, where the soldiers had repeatedly to climb down from the parapet to the track by rope, and haul themselves up the bank again by another rope. Finally, they all threw grenades from the bridge at a target to complete that part of their training. Eventually, having been woken in the middle of the night to go and attack the engine and its train, the soldiers are confronted by the general who sent them on their training, arriving at the station from the direction of the railway cottages over the field via a jeep. They are told that their training is over a week early – they need to leave for Germany tomorrow ...

Lee Marvin and soldiers relax between scenes for *The Dirty Dozen* in 1984.

## Bullshot

This film, made in 1983, was a spoof of the swashbuckling 'Bulldog Drummond' series, and it incorporated all the right things: a secret formula, evil German villains, a ditzy blonde heroine and a 'terribly British' hero. The scientist father of Rosemary, the heroine, has been kidnapped for his secret formula, and Rosemary attempts to make a getaway by train with her half of the formula in a locket around her neck. She is travelling in carriage No. 6575, somewhere along the Bluebell line, hauled by Schools Class No. 928, when she is accosted in her compartment by a Catholic priest and a nun – the evil German villain and villainess, of course. It is the work of a moment to steal her locket and throw her out of the carriage door to her death. Or so they thought ...

Here the stunt double took over, as, working on a specially erected platform beside the train, she made her way along the outside of the carriage to the next compartment to rap on the door with her umbrella. The compartment is occupied by a blind Scotsman (Billy Connolly), an ex-serviceman from the regiment of Bullshot Crummond, the hero of our story. He hears the knock, assumes that he must have arrived at Horsted Keynes (actually referred to as such in the film) and opens the door, flattening Rosemary against the side of the carriage and falling down the embankment. The stretch of embankment used for the shot at Waterworks Bridge had been meticulously cleared of brambles and roots beforehand; the stuntman was wearing a kilt!

The train arrives at Horsted Keynes with the hapless Rosemary still clinging to the open carriage door. As it draws to a halt in the platform, the stationmaster (Ted Moult) admonishes her for opening the door while the train is still in motion.

After a whirlwind of improbable adventures, hero Bullshot and heroine Rosemary parachute down to earth together from a small plane, landing, fortuitously, on the arm of a signal specially erected by Waterworks Bridge. As C Class No. 592 approaches with its train, Bullshot calculates that the signal arm will drop at the precise moment that his friend passes along the road underneath the bridge in a vintage car on the route of the London to Brighton vehicle run ...

More work for the stunt artists as they drop from the signal into the passing car, where Bullshot takes over the driving from his friend. As he so reasonably points out, having now saved the secret formula (and of course, the world), rescued the professor and his daughter and defeated the evil villains, there was no reason why he couldn't end the day by winning the London to Brighton run.

*Right*: A kilted Bullshot (Billy Connolly) flattens Rosemary against the train door.

*Below*: Bullshot's stunt double jumps from the train.

# 7

# The 1980s: Television

## The Decade that Taste Forgot

The launch of Channel 4 in 1982 was the beginning of a new era for multi-channel television, and the opening night of the channel on 2 November had included a film about a young handicapped boy, a pivotal scene of which was filmed on Town Place Bridge between Sheffield Park and Horsted Keynes as a train passed under it.

The Big Three (BBC1, BBC2 and ITV) were starting to face competition from more directions than one. With the video recorder coming onto the scene, and these were the days when nobody knew whether the VHS or Betamax format would eventually win the market share.

The music video entered the fray, although it has since faded from view, and the Bluebell made over forty adverts and pop videos during the 1980s, making it the busiest decade ever for TV advertising.

TV was a bigger customer than film, and there was a lot of it. Documentaries, popular programmes, children's TV, comedy series and serials all made their appearance. The centenary of the birth of Agatha Christie fell in 1990, and the last few years of the 1980s saw a proliferation of Christie murder mysteries and the first of the long-running *Poirot* series. A couple of decades later, David Suchet, who played Poirot, once commented that he had been visiting Horsted Keynes station in its various guises for twenty years.

Several big TV personalities of the decade graced our stations during those years – some of them yet to be discredited. Kenny Everett came to Horsted Keynes to film a sketch for *The Kenny Everett Video Show* (later renamed *The Kenny Everett Video Cassette*), which centred around five skeletons dressed in business suits in a first-class compartment – they had been waiting for a train since 1959.

Harry Secombe, who found fame in *The Goon Show*, took a career change in later years and presented *Highway*, a television version of the Radio Four programme *Down Your Way*. He travelled around the country talking to locals about places of interest in the area and singing songs, whether or not the locals wanted him to. He came to Horsted Keynes in September 1988, where he spoke to superintendent Bernard Holden about the railway and Revd Mark Hill Tout about St Giles' Church and the village. It happened to be

Harry Secombe's sixty-seventh birthday, and while at the station he was presented with a cake by the TVS film crew. He then sang 'Find the Silver Lining', which turned out to be appropriate, as locomotive *Stepney* failed and the Adams Radial Tank No. 488 had to be substituted at the last minute.

Comedian Harry Enfield is well known for his sharply observed characters, whose catch phrases were repeated throughout the land – Kevin the teenager's 'I hate you! It's not fair!' echoes to this day. Harry came to Horsted Keynes in 1989 to film a spoof of *The South Bank Show*. It was entitled *Norbert Smith* and presented by Melvyn Bragg, playing himself as the presenter of the show, a man well accustomed to interviewing actors about their fascinating lives. He interviewed the eighty-year-old Norbert Smith about his career, and several film clips were shown, all bearing an uncanny resemblance to the major films of the last few decades. Harry Enfield, also the writer, came to Horsted Keynes to play the young Norbert in the 1940s. He was departing on a train hauled by Standard No. 75027, waving to the girl he left behind him, and also filmed some scenes in the 1940s refreshment room.

More television comedy came with a visit from Mel Smith and Griff Rhys Jones who, following their success as one half of the satirical sketch show *Not the Nine O'Clock News*, came to the railway to film a sketch for their duo series *Alas Smith and Jones*. The sketch involved a gag about mobile phones and involved Bluebell volunteers dressed as business travellers, a live cow on the platform and a 'dressed down' Mel Smith. Mel and Griff are talking on mobiles opposite each other in the buffet car and it then transpires they are talking to each other when Mel says, 'Where's the figures?' and Griff hands him the file. All the extras were handed dummy mobile phones so as the camera pans everyone in the carriage is on the phone. With twenty-first-century smartphones and texting the sketch now seems very dated.

Comedian Harry Enfield is impressed with this destination namesake!

Mel Smith and a microphone outside Horsted Keynes station.

Several popular general interest programmes turned up at the Bluebell, including *Timewatch*'s 'True Story of the Roman Arena' (BBC 2 arts programme) and Anneka Rice's *Treasure Hunt* – the latter starting at the railway for a Sussex-based episode as contestants are given the next clue in the studio by anchorman Kenneth Kendall.

The BBC programme *Q.E.D.* filmed an investigation into the famous Piltdown Man – when the 'discovery' of a prehistoric male skull in the 1900s turned out to be a hoax. It was filmed, as many of these things are, in the style of a Sherlock Holmes mystery, with Holmes played by Hugh Fraser (soon to return to Horsted Keynes, in its guise as Styles St Mary, as Poirot's sidekick, Captain Hastings) and Dr Watson played by Ronald Fraser. The North London Tank No. 58850 drew a train into Horsted Keynes to be boarded by the two detectives on their way to look into the problem. The film crew had forgotten to bring their smoke canister, a vital piece of kit when filming anything to do with a steam engine, so the engine had to provide its own special effects. A steam lance was attached to the steam heat pipe in order to bathe Holmes and Watson in the obligatory clouds of steam as they set off for the heart of Sussex, Piltdown being just a few miles from Sheffield Park.

## Children's TV – *Thomas & Friends*

Children's television was expanding from its customary slot of just an hour or two a day, and there was more of it than ever before – whether it was better quality was debatable. Thomas the Tank Engine epitomised the 1980s. It was a bit of an unlikely hit, based on a series of stories written by a reverend decades earlier about 'old-fashioned steam trains' to get his young son off to sleep, but it took off in a big way. The original Revd Awdry stories were read by Ringo Starr and brought to life by what was little more than an animated train set, but it was immensely popular. Kids love steam trains (always have, always will). In April 1987 Ringo visited the railway to spend the day with two young children with leukaemia who had requested to meet him, in his capacity as the voice of 'Thomas' and friends in the TV series. *Stepney the Bluebell Engine* (starring as itself as it was in one of the original books) pulled the observation car with Ringo and the children aboard as he read them one of their favourite stories.

Children's TV was still a long way from the dedicated channels of today, and although it wasn't possible to watch it all day every day, Saturday morning television was starting to take off, and the Bluebell featured on these programmes a couple of times.

*Stepney,* the railway's most popular engine with children, made another appearance with the Great Northern Railway saloon for *Saturday Superstore.* Presenter Keith 'Cheggers' Chegwin interviewed Traffic Manager John Hill about the running of the railway, and travelled in the saloon carriage with some children from the local primary school, St Giles' in Horsted Keynes. He later 'missed' the train from Sheffield Park to Horsted Keynes and chased it as far as the bottom of Freshfield Bank on a pump trolley.

'Thomas' narrator Ringo Starr visited in April 1987 and met with some young Thomas fans and *Stepney the Bluebell engine*, which was one of Revd Awdry's well-loved titles in the 'Thomas' series.

Keith 'Cheggers' Chegwin interviews Bluebell Traffic Manager John Hill about the running of the railway for *Saturday Superstore*.

## TV Documentaries

Bluebell was the backdrop for several documentaries during the 1980s, some investigating events in the local area, some with a broader interest, and also appeared in the biographies of Oscar Wilde, Ken Russell and Princess Diana.

Horsted Keynes appeared as Haslemere in 1984, the scene of a pivotal meeting between Captain Scott and fellow explorer Wilson, which ultimately led to the ill-fated expedition to the South Pole in 1912, in a programme for Central TV entitled *The Last Place on Earth*. In a good example of the station's versatility, it went on to play Liverpool Street station in 1985 for the BBC documentary *The Secret of Life*. It related the discovery of DNA (deoxyribonucleic acid) in the 1940s in Cambridge. DNA is the substance making up chains of genetic information that determines everything about us in a 'double helix' spiral, and, at the time of filming, the working title was *Double Helix*, later changed to *The Secret of Life*. The discovery was a huge leap forward in scientific knowledge, on a par with the discovery that people had different blood groups.

## Adverts and Fashion Shoots

The 1980s was the most prolific decade ever for adverts, most of which were mundane bread-and-butter stuff, including some relics from previous decades that were starting to look old-fashioned. The International Wool Federation, Thomson Directories, Avon Cosmetics, Reader's Digest, Princes Potted Meat Spread, and a James Last album were among those that would have been familiar with more than one generation. However, modern technology was creeping in with adverts for Cellnet portable phones ('portable' being, in today's terms, a generous epithet) and Sony video cameras.

Most of the fashion shoots in those days were a little staid and old maidish, probably as befitted a steam railway. Robin wool knitting patterns, *Woman & Home* magazine and Burberry put in an appearance; Burberry has since been revamped as an upmarket and 'high end' fashion house, but in the 1980s it was mainly associated with raincoats. The tone was raised with the jewellers Asprey of Bond Street and *Harpers & Queen* magazine, bringing a bit of class to the railway.

In May 1985, an elaborate set was built at Horsted Keynes for an advert for the British Motorcycle Association. It was intended to depict train travel as dull, drab, dreary and fraught with difficulties (and that was way before privatisation) in contrast to the excitement and freedom of motorcycling. At the crucial moment, the alternative to British Rail refused to start.

The new Ford Escort was advertised as a 'family car that forgives mistakes'. You could leave it out in the cold and expect it to start in the morning, miss a turning and do a U-turn, and load it up with large amounts of luggage. An example of this last scenario was filmed in the forecourt of Horsted Keynes station, where mother-in-law has just arrived on the train with a trolley load ('staying long, mother?').

In the days before sat nav was invented as the most ingenious way of causing chaos and confusion on Britain's roads, the AA advertised its services as an organisation that did much more than mending cars. The catchphrase was that they 'know a man who can'. In November 1986 a patient female giraffe called Vicky was brought to the low-arched New Road Bridge just south of Horsted Keynes station in an open truck, where her neck reared up against the 8-foot 9-inch restriction sign. She played the part of 'Gerald', and the truck driver was filmed asking a passer-by, 'How can I get Gerald to Chester Zoo without going under any low bridges?' The passer-by can't tell him, but the AA 'will know a man who can'. The filming of this short clip took an entire morning (with the road closed), and everyone from the village policeman upwards turned out to watch. Vicky was sustained by a bucket of bananas while there was much positioning of lights and shields before her neck would show up against the sun-dappled bricks of the bridge.

The road is closed to traffic at New Road Bridge, Horsted Keynes, as 'Gerald' the Giraffe can't fit under the bridge on a journey to Chester Zoo for an AA advertisement.

## The Pop Video

Vinyl record sleeve artwork came and went – a young Elton John having used Sheffield Park station as the backdrop to his third album *Tumbleweed Connection* in 1970 – and then in the 1980s the pop video came and went, and was very much a product of its time.

Several pop videos used the Bluebell as a location, including bands such as The Roonies and Hipsway and singers Rick Springfield and Al Jarreau, as well as Morris and the Minors' smash hit 'Trainspotter in Love' (no, me neither).

Sheena Easton's hit 'My Baby Takes the Morning Train' was well known at the time, and an obvious candidate for the Bluebell – others less so.

In November 1983 Tracey Ullman filmed a video for her song 'Move Over Darling', featuring almost as much of *Stepney* as it did of her. The video has a very 1950s ballroom flavour, and opens with Tracey's beau driving *Stepney*, rushing to get back in time for an evening of ballroom dancing, shaving in the cab during the journey. He meets Tracey, clad in a puff of pink ballgown, and they go off to the dance in a motorbike and sidecar. They return, proudly bearing the trophy, to Sheffield Park station, where they both board *Stepney* and drive off with the train into the distance, waving from the cab.

Sheena Easton 'takes the morning train' in 1980.

Tracey Ullman in a ballgown for filming the video for her hit 'Move over Darling' in 1983.

The Pet Shop Boys (Neil Tennant and Chris Lowe) became the Menagerie Boys in October 1987 when they made a video for their Elvis cover of 'Always on my Mind', which involved a live zebra and a herd of cattle on the platform at Horsted Keynes, along with a giant inflatable fried egg, although the latter didn't make the final cut.

Apropos of nothing, the zebra was led across the foot crossing onto the platform and loaded into a brake van, hauled by Terrier No. 72 *Fenchurch*. The Pet Shop Boys were seated on a station bench and the train was required to 'whisper past' (the director's words), leaving a mist of steam to melt away in front of the singers. The first time, the 'whisper' of steam was completely inaudible and the next time it totally obliterated the scene, but after a few takes the desired effect was produced.

# 8

# The 1980s: TV Serials

## Comedies

### It Ain't Half Hot Mum

The very popular BBC TV comedy that followed the misfortunes of a Royal Artillery concert party entertaining the troops in India during the Second World War. Forever living by the creed 'the show must go on', they were continually hampered in their efforts by a sergeant major (Windsor Davies) who was determined, against all the odds, to turn them into 'real men' and proper soldiers. They were all under the half-hearted command of a

The cast of BBC TV comedy *It Ain't Half Hot Mum* pose at Horsted Keynes for their final 'demob' episode.

couple of upper-class 'silly ass' officers who did nothing at all and in the company of whom the sergeant major was forced to conceal his irritation.

In July 1981 the entire concert party visited Horsted Keynes station to film the final 'demob' scenes for the very last episode of the long-running series, transmitted on 3 September that year. It was a lovely summer's day, and both cast and crew were a little demob happy ...

## If You Go Down in the Woods Today

Eric Sykes was one of those comedians that was 'never off the telly' in the late 1970s and early 1980s. He made several films, some silent (*The Plank*) and some talkies. In this one, filmed in 1980, Sykes is a hapless scoutmaster taking a troupe of cub scouts camping in the woods, back in the day when a grown man in a woggle and shorts could be portrayed going camping with a group of small boys without necessarily causing a sharp intake of breath.

Arriving at Twittering station (Horsted Keynes) by train, Sykes unloads his cubs and their handcart from the brake van in which they have been travelling. He asks the stationmaster the way to Tanglewood and receives a dubious reply. 'All sorts of odd goings on in Tanglewood – you don't want to go there. All sorts of things going into the woods and only these coming out ...' he nods at some coffins stacked outside the buffet. The coffins are picked up to be loaded onto a train, and Sykes' scout whistle turns up underneath one of them. He examines it closely, shakes it, blows it experimentally, and the train in Platform 3, hauled by the Adams Tank No. 488, departs prematurely, the stationmaster trapped on board. Sykes and his cub scouts disappear with their handcart, off for their inevitable series of disastrous adventures.

Eric Sykes plays a hapless scoutmaster in the film *If You Go Down in the Woods Today*.

## Dramas

Horsted Keynes was the backdrop for the following biographical dramas.

### *A Voyage Round My Father* (Thames TV)
This was based on the autobiographical account of the last years of writer John Mortimer's father, Clifford Mortimer. John Mortimer's most famous creation, *Rumpole of the Bailey*, owed something to his creator's time at the bar, and Mortimer Sr was also a lawyer. A wheelchair-bound Laurence Olivier played Clifford Mortimer during the latter years, when he struggled with increasing blindness, but still continued to appear in court.

Laurence Olivier in Thames TV's *A Voyage Round My Father*.

## Portrait of a Marriage (BBC)

During the years towards the end of the First World War and into the twentieth century, government minister Harold Nicolson and his wife Vita Sackville-West were among the beautiful people of the Bloomsbury Group and appeared to have an idyllic marriage – on the surface, anyway. Behind closed doors, things are not what they seem. Everything seems to come to a head when Harold requires medical treatment for a certain delicate condition, necessitating Vita also receive treatment. He is forced to admit that he has been sleeping with men, which opens a can of worms.

When Vita's childhood friend, Violet Keppel, comes to stay, the two of them embark upon a passionate and reckless love affair and run away to Paris for several months. Vita seriously considers leaving Harold to live with Violet for good, a move that, in the 1920s, would have lost her most of her friends and her position in society and left her an outcast. Harold and Vita manage to weather the storm, but with consequences that resonate throughout their lives.

Horsted Keynes plays a key role as Sevenoaks, the nearest station to Harold and Vita's home at Sissinghurst.

## Walter

This story, based on the book by David Cook, was scheduled to be shown on the opening night of new TV station Channel Four on Tuesday 2 November 1982, so the Bluebell could claim some kudos for appearing on that auspicious occasion – although I don't recall that it did. *Walter,* made by Central Television ATV, tells the story of a man born with a mental illness, and the scene filmed on Freshfield Bank in September 1982 was a flashback to an incident in his childhood that had affected him very deeply. His mother suffered from depression, and, one day in the 1940s, with desperate intentions, took her son to a railway bridge. She sat him on the parapet, preparatory to pushing him off in the path of an oncoming train, thus ending his troubles, and perhaps her own. She held back at the last moment, unable to bring herself to do it, but the incident made an indelible impression upon Walter and remained with him for the rest of his life.

Walter's mother was played by Barbara Jefford and adult Walter by Ian McKellan, and the scene of the incident was Town Place Farm Bridge. They approached it from the footpath as the Q1 No. 33001 was timed to pass under it from Freshfield. They have to run to reach the bridge in time, and Walter is helped up onto the parapet, where his mother holds him as the train passes underneath, enveloping the bridge and its occupants in smoke and steam. Once the train has passed and the smoke has cleared, they are both still there. Walter's mother helps him down and they walk away, back along the footpath.

## Hannay

In 1987 a sequel to *The Thirty-Nine Steps* was made by Thames TV, starring Robert Powell, which followed the fortunes of the regiment featured in the film. One by one, the men of the regiment receive cryptic quotes from Shakespeare, hinting at their imminent demise. Sure as eggs is eggs, one by one they are bumped off. For Hannay, attempting to get to the bottom of the mystery, time is running out.

At the station, a member of the blighted regiment boards the train, following receipt of his warning Shakespearian quote, hoping to escape retribution by rail, with a policemen

Actor Robert Powell is Hannay. Robert recalled visiting the railway with Ken Russell in 1972.

seeing him off and warning him to take care. Filming took place from the lineside and on the train as it travelled between Sheffield Park and Horsted Keynes, the gentleman on the train neatly murdered in his seat en route. The final scene shot at the railway was of the train hurtling into a tunnel in dramatic fashion; no railway murder is quite the same without a tunnel. In 1987 we had no tunnel (yet), so Leamland Bridge had to do.

## The Detectives of the Golden Age

Sir Arthur Conan Doyle started it, with the first fictional detective of them all. Over 130 years later, Sherlock Holmes, Dr Watson and Moriarty are still appearing in adaptations of his stories and much of the great detective has found its way into our language and culture. The list of actors who have portrayed the leading roles is a long one, and in the 1980s Jeremy Brett as Holmes and Edward Hardwicke as Watson had a go at bringing them to life in a TV series that was very faithful to the original stories, sticking to the plots as written and using much of the original dialogue. We saw them at Horsted Keynes a few times, always in character – Jeremy Brett once strolled up to the engine while not 'on set' and made a show of examining it as Holmes would have done, without a hint of irony.

The 1920s and 1930s were described as the golden age of women's detective fiction, producing such writers as Agatha Christie, Margery Allingham and Dorothy L. Sayers. Books by Christie and Allingham were made into TV series during the late 1980s and early 1990s, using the Bluebell as a location. Hercule Poirot, played by David Suchet, was to spend a quarter of a century returning to Horsted Keynes station in his quest to play the Belgian detective in every story that the author ever wrote about him.

### The Girl in the Train
Filmed during a hectic few days in November 1981 when the ever-versatile Horsted Keynes station masqueraded as Waterloo, Petersfield, Rowlands Castle, Liss, Portsmouth Harbour, Woking, Wanborough and Ash. Whoever that girl was, she certainly spent a lot of time in the train.

## The Sunningdale Mystery

This used a range of locations around the railway. From Sheffield Park station, the unit moved to Sheffield Park House, and from Horsted Keynes station to the Martindale Centre (the church hall) in the village of Horsted Keynes and Horsted Mill. At that time, the water mill, mentioned in the Domesday Book, was being restored to working order.

## The Secret Adversary

This featured a train hauled by C Class No. 592, carrying such distinguished passengers as Honor Blackman, Peter Barkworth, George Baker and Donald Houston.

## The Baker Street Boys

Sherlockian spin-offs are nothing new, and in 1982 scenes were shot for a film about the infamous Baker Street Boys. Well-known characters, they were the gang of street urchins employed by Holmes (on a zero-hours contract) to assist him in his enquiries. The eyes and ears of London's seamier underside, they were able to infiltrate places that a gentleman, even with Holmes' talent for disguise, could not. The locations used were Barcombe Mills station, Sheffield Park House and Freshfield Bank, where a bomb is placed on the railway line and the train, hauled by No. 592, almost comes to grief.

## 'The Greek Interpreter'

In April 1983 an episode for Granada TV's *The Adventures of Sherlock Holmes* series was filmed around Horsted Keynes, the various scenes taking a week to film. Coach No. 6575 was cocooned in blackout material for several days while the interior shots were filmed, and the interior of the Great Northern saloon was converted into a first-class buffet car, on a train where the characters flee for their lives. To add drama, scenes of the departing train were filmed at night. Platform 3 at Horsted Keynes was Herne Hill, while Platform 4 became Dover, and No. 592 with the Metropolitan coaches departed energetically towards Leamland Bridge. The usual atmospheric red glow from the firebox visible on a passing train was supplemented by the firing of submarine flares, which may have added to the dramatic effect, but also temporarily blinded everyone in the vicinity.

## Hercule Poirot's Casebook

In 1987 David Suchet, as Agatha Christie's Belgian detective Hercule Poirot, was at the height of his popularity. In July of that year, he was at Horsted Keynes filming night scenes inside blacked-out carriages, and the arrival of the detective in the station forecourt. He draws up outside the station in a car driven by his friend and sidekick Captain Hastings, holding onto his hat with his silver-topped stick in characteristic fashion.

'Are you sure you won't let me drive you?' Hastings asks.

'The train has one advantage over the car,' replies Poirot, having had experience of previous journeys with his friend. 'It won't run out of coal.'

At this point the Standard Class 4 No. 75027, on the service train, drowned the remainder of his lines by departing with the drain cocks open. Once it had gone, Suchet added, aside, 'But they do have a terrible sense of timing.'

David Suchet (Poirot), Hugh Fraser (Captain Hastings) and accomplice await the next scene outside Horsted Keynes station.

The Q Class No. 541 was hauling the filming train. Under orders from the director, the train passed over Waterworks Bridge making as much noise and black smoke that could be managed, blowing off and with the cocks open.

## Campion: 'Dancers in Mourning'

Margery Allingham's detective of the 1920s and 1930s, Campion, was brought to life on the screen by Peter Davison in 1989. Horsted Keynes featured prominently with two highly dramatic explosion scenes filmed at the station. The location manager had spent some time ferreting around in the locality, and scenes were also filmed at Kingscote station and around the hamlet of Birch Grove along the quiet country lanes. One scene was intended as a picturesque one of Campion's car splashing through the small ford, but, due to a long spell of hot, dry weather the stream had to be damned to produce any flow of water at all.

Horsted Keynes station was, in turn, Birley and Broadbridge. At Birley, the U Class No. 1618 stood in the station with its train, the ticket inspector stood outside his booth contemplating infinity, crates of vegetables awaited loading and pigeons fluttered and cooed nearby – the epitome of a quiet country station. Or not. A bomb had been planted in the ticket booth, and the explosion was elaborately set up so that at the moment of detonation the lid flew off the pigeon basket and the somewhat disgruntled birds rose in a body and flew up to take refuge in the station canopy. Getting them down again proved to be more time-consuming than setting up the explosion.

# 9

# The 1990s

## A Decade of Variety

As far as the railway was concerned, the TV serial that defined the decade was Agatha Christie's *Poirot*, with David Suchet turning up for the railway scenes needed in five episodes. The Bluebell also appeared in around twenty films during this decade and was a major player in two of them: the Monty Python-inspired version of *The Wind in the Willows* and the TV remake of *The Railway Children*.

Canned Guinness was beginning to take off in America, and the marketing people decided that they wanted to get away from the 'tits, bums and beaches' (their words) approach of American beer advertising, and so they came up with the old 'trains in tunnels' routine. A couple travelling by train open a can of Guinness, which froths up courtesy of the newly invented 'widgit' inside, the froth turning to steam and loco No. 75027 comes thundering out of the can – which is really a tunnel. The film crew spent four bleak January days filming this, while the train was up and down the line and in and out of the tunnel like a fiddler's elbow, complemented by some dramatic lighting effects and plenty of escaping steam.

Pop videos, having enjoyed brief popularity, were on the wane again, and only two were made at Bluebell in the 1990s. One was for the Reggae Philharmonic Orchestra and the other a cover version of 'Unchained Melody', which featured two actors from popular TV series of the time *Soldier Soldier*, Robson Green and Jerome Flynn. Horsted Keynes became Milford Junction for an evening, with a train hauled by No. 847 drawing into it, and scenes from this shoot were cut in with original scenes from the film *Brief Encounter*.

## *Black Beauty*

Anna Sewell, born in 1820, severely injured her ankles as a child and spent much of her life laid up and unable to walk. When her family lived in Lancing, it was Anna's duty to drive her father to and from Shoreham station every day in the pony chaise, and here her interest in the welfare of horses was born. She was particularly concerned about the plight of cabmen and cab horses, and was inspired to write her 'little book' by an incident related to her by a cab driver. *Black Beauty* was published in 1877, and she lived just long enough to enjoy its success.

*Black Beauty* tells the life story of a horse, written from his perspective, from his happy colthood in a meadow, through hard times as a London cab horse, to a final rescue by an old friend and eventual happy retirement. The emphasis was always on the subjugation of horses to their owner's whims and their complete impotence to influence their own fate, and Anna drew attention to several cruel practices of the time, such as the 'leading rein' used by the upper classes to force up their horses' heads.

In September 1993 Warner Brothers visited to film scenes for an adaptation of this classic novel, along the lineside and at Horsted station. On the first day of filming, a road had been built leading down to the railway line at the top of Freshfield Bank. The H Class No. 263, hauling a small branch-line train, passed 'Black Beauty' and his rider, in an early scene when the young horse was being trained to cope with passing trains. 'Beauty' was supposed to startle at the sound of the train, but, after a number of takes, the horse playing the part had become so used to it that he refused to show any signs of anxiety.

On the second day, Horsted station was painstakingly transformed. A coal yard was set up, complete with coal office on the old cattle dock, and the pile of ballast that happened to be there at the time was sprayed black to represent the coal. The station forecourt was crowded and bustling with coal carts, horses and traps and Victorians from all walks of life, some of whom bore a passing resemblance to Bluebell volunteers. It was an emotional scene for 'Beauty', as the family with whom he, 'Merrylegs' and 'Ginger' had shared some happy times was moving away due to the illness of the mistress, and, having delivered the family to the railway station, the three horses were to be sold and split up; the scenes at the station were the last of the happy times.

Away from the station, a 'road' was made up next to the line at Freshfield Bank for the lineside scenes in *Black Beauty*.

## The Return of Sam McCloud

The fame of the Bluebell Railway seems to have spread by the 1990s, and a number of films by international companies were made here, most of which were only shown abroad, and, in the era before the Internet, Amazon and Netflix, never seen by the Bluebell staff and volunteers who worked on or appeared in them. Two French, two American, one Canadian and one Chinese crew made films with the Bluebell as a background, not always with an English setting.

In the American film *The Return of Sam McCloud*, McCloud's nephew is murdered in England and he crosses the pond in order to apprehend the murderer. The filming took place overnight aboard a train hauled by the U Class No. 1618. Several stuntmen were called upon to leap from the running board of one of the carriages while the train was in motion, and one of them missed his footing and ended his night with a broken ankle.

## A Ghost in Monte Carlo

Not long after the filming for *The Return of Sam McCloud*, scenes were shot at Horsted Keynes for an adaptation of a Barbara Cartland story, *A Ghost in Monte Carlo*, Horsted Keynes becoming Monte Carlo station in 1883. The Metropolitan coaches featured in the film, with an engine on either end – No. 96 *Normandy* and Adams tank No. 488. Jason Connery starred in the film and ran along the platform as the train was about to depart, desperately searching for someone inside it. He slipped on the platform (not in the screenplay), put his arm out to save himself and plunged his fist through the (closed) window of the GNR directors' saloon. He was taken to the hospital for repair, and returned later to complete the shot, the saloon window also repaired and his bandages heavily disguised.

## Where Angels Fear to Tread

At this time Merchant Ivory was still making adaptations of E. M. Forster novels, and a substantial amount of time was spent filming scenes for *Where Angels Fear to Tread*, starring the usual suspects, Rupert Graves and Helena Bonham Carter. Yet another exposé of uptight, buttoned-up Edwardian morals, it tells the story of a woman who 'gets into trouble' with an Italian man, Gino, and then dies in Italy giving birth to his baby – events that her family is anxious to conceal. Horsted Keynes features several times during the to-ing and fro-ing between England and Italy, and then forms the background to the pivotal final scene, at night. The North London tank No. 2650 and its train departs to leave Helena Bonham Carter and Rupert Graves talking while walking along the platform. They have been to Italy as friends of the family in an attempt to bring the baby home – unsuccessfully, as Gino insists, quite unreasonably, of course, on bringing up his own child. They enter the buffet and Bonham Carter reveals how she herself had fallen in love with Gino, as they look out of the buffet windows across the darkened and deserted platforms.

## Halcyon Days

*Halcyon Days* was a film made for showing in France in 1994, and utilised one of the longest freight trains that the Bluebell has ever marshalled at twenty-three vehicles. Filming took three days and two nights, during which the Q1 Class C1 was in steam and working constantly. The film was set in France in 1938 and told a dark story of murder and incest, concerning the killing of a boy and the involvement of his twin brother. Horsted Keynes represented a quiet French station at the dead of night, following heavy rain, through which the Q1 hauled a freight train comprising flat trucks, vans and wagons, some loaded with strange shapes covered in camouflage netting, and military vehicles roped down. This train rumbled slowly past in the background of the shot (a couple embracing on a railway platform), the last few wagons timed to roll past as 'cut' was called.

## Voices From a Locked Room

Horsted Keynes station was nicknamed 'Bumsup Junction' for a night shoot in October 1994, part of a Canadian film *Voices From a Locked Room*. The film is a biography of the schizophrenic composer Peter Warlord and set in England in the 1920s. Most of the film was shot in Montreal, the only scenes actually shot in England being some London streets, the River Thames and the Bluebell scenes. When the director first discussed the proposed filming with Bluebell Operations Manager Martin Miller, he had mentioned some 'bum shots', which Martin, in his innocence, had assumed to be some filming jargon. But no. The hero and heroine, travelling home from visiting his parents, made good use of the privacy of their first-class carriage. As the train passes slowly through the station, one of the blinds flips up, revealing to the passengers waiting on the platform a naked female posterior pressed against the window.

S15 Class No. 847 hauled the train, and carriage No. 6575 was the one upon which all eyes were turned. Several volunteers were used as extras to ride on the train (where they saw nothing of the action). My son Henry (nine at the time) played the part of a boy with a yo-yo standing on the platform and I was his mother, putting my hands over his eyes as the bottom flashed past. Unfortunately, it was one of those films made in the 1990s never to be seen in the UK.

## The Young Indiana Jones

This follows the fortunes of the adventurer during his childhood travels around the globe with his parents. In May 1994 a busy day was spent at Horsted Keynes, turning it into Kyhuebo in Russia, Paris, Nice, Le Havre and Peking. The film was set (more or less) in 1910 and used the C Class No. 592, with the family travelling in the director's saloon.

The end result was something of a continuity nightmare. As the Jones family travelled from India to China, a variety of trains and engines was depicted steaming along through the Indian, then Chinese, landscape, with the family always in the same saloon – which of course wasn't on any of the trains. As they arrive in Peking, the train is suddenly hauled

Peking market comes to Horsted Keynes station dock for *The Young Indiana Jones* in May 1994.

by an SR 'yankee tank' at the Longmoor Military Railway, with a diesel shunter clearly visible in the background. As they travel through Russia, the train of Southern coaches is hauled by the Q1, with Russia in the background and family Jones still aboard the same saloon, mysteriously invisible on the actual train. The Q1 changes to a Russian engine and back to the Q1 a few times during the journey, apart from a couple of brief flashes when the frames of C Class No. 592 appear, paving the way for the train to pull in to Kyhuebo station hauled by No. 592.

## *The Enchanted Hill*

Filmed in October 1995, this was another offering for foreign screens. It told the story of American newspaper tycoon William Randolph Hurst, and Horsted Keynes became Limoges in France at the turn of the century. As a child, Hurst was taken on a 'lightning tour' of Europe by his mother, and once again Horsted Keynes and a Bluebell train (the Pullman coaches hauled by the C Class No. 592) were called upon to represent several countries. Each Pullman car was dressed to represent the interior of a train in one of three different countries – France, Belgium, and Switzerland.

The train entered the station several times with passengers boarding and alighting – the film was shown only in America.

# Going Loco: Steam Sunday

During the autumn of 1990, Channel 4 showed a series of classic railway films and contemporary documentaries under the theme of 'Going Loco'. The series was introduced from the Bluebell and showed various clips from the engine shed, museum, Horsted Keynes station, and the footplate of No. 96 *Normandy*. Frontman DJ Mike Read was also present, making a trailer to promote Steam Sunday from the footplate of Adams Radial tank No. 488.

Steam Sunday was a day of musical entertainment and railway-related fun from Horsted Keynes station. It got underway with a set from the band Instant Sunshine, although the sunshine didn't last – being an English summer day, it soon began to rain. The star of the show was 1960s singer Joe Brown, who was once a fireman on the Eastern Region at Plaistow depot and worked many trains before taking up a more lucrative career as a musician. He played a few sets with his band and crammed onto the footplate of No. 323 *Bluebell* with a seemingly impossible number of children to show them how it worked.

Other celebrities were present on the day and appeared in film clips in between the live takes. The stars of the 1972 film *The Railway Children* were there to reminisce, and Sally Thomsett, who played Phyllis, was shown revisiting Oakworth on the Keighley & Worth Valley Railway and meeting volunteer guard Mr Mitchell, who had appeared as the guard in the film. Back at Horsted Keynes, Sally, Dinah Sheridan (mother), Gary Warren (Peter), Sally Thomsett (Phyllis), and Bernard Cribbins (Perks) gathered for a cosy chat about the making of *The Railway Children,* then eighteen years previously.

Pianist Jools Holland and Joe Brown's daughter, singer Sam Brown, also provided musical entertainment, getting very wet in the process.

Presenter Mike Read interviews four of the cast of the original 1970 EMI film *The Railway Children* with Bernard Cribbins and Dinah Sheriden (seated), with Sally Thomsett and Gary Warren standing behind, for Channel 4's *Steam Sunday*.

## The Wind in the Willows

In 1995 the Bluebell was the scene for a new feature film version of the classic story first written in 1908. It was directed by ex-Python Terry Jones, who wanted to build up the brief railway scene in the book into an exciting and action-packed few minutes, and the unit spent three weeks at the railway filming the scenes.

The original book follows the adventures of four animals of the British countryside: short-sighted and naive Mole, the sensible Water Rat, wise, retiring Badger, and the ebullient, posturing Toad. Toad is prone to crazes, and his latest one, for the motorcar, lands him in big trouble (twenty years in prison, no less) for the crimes of stealing a car, dangerous driving, and 'cheek'.

He manages to escape dressed as a washerwoman and makes for the nearest station. There he discovers that he has no money to buy a ticket, and bursts into tears. The kindly engine driver

*Above left*: Toad (Terry Jones) disguised as a washerwoman.

*Above right*: Eric Idle (Ratty).

takes pity on him and allows him to ride on the footplate, even though it is 'against company regulations'. The forces of the law, also against accepted railway practice, follow aboard a light engine, and Toad reveals his identity to the engine driver and throws himself on his mercy. The driver agrees to let Toad jump off at the end of a long tunnel, and then drives on with the police still chasing him, so that Toad can escape. The main changes to the story consisted of the police travelling in the train behind Toad's engine, the driver falling off the engine, and Toad driving it and crashing it after the other animals had detached it from the train.

Toad was played by Terry Jones, with more than a hint of pantomime dame; Ratty was played by another ex-Python, Eric Idle; Mole by comedian Steve Coogan; the engine driver by Bernard Hill; and the pursuing prison warder by Don Henderson.

In order to simulate the speed of 106 mph that Toad managed to reach with the C Class, the film of the light engine was considerably sped up, then an explosion was set up at the crash site for the engine finally coming off the road, and the cameras cut to the wreckage of the C Class in the trees and Toad crawling out from underneath it.

An accurate wooden and plastic replica of the back of the tender was constructed for the scene and placed by the lineside, buried in the trees, much admired by all the Bluebell members who saw it.

In Terry Jones' final scenes as Toad at the railway, he was filmed crawling out from beneath the wreckage, surrounded by blasts of steam, dishevelled and much the worse for wear, but ready to fight another day. Meanwhile, the runaway train slows down and comes to a stand, and Ratty and Mole climb down. Mole has had enough and decides to go home, digging a hole by the railway line.

*The Wind in the Willows* was released in 1996.

Ratty and Mole (Eric Idle and Steve Coogan) are 'stranded' after the train splitting scene.

# 10

# The Railway Children

Edith Nesbit's book *The Railway Children,* written in 1904, is the most famous of all her children's books, and has become one of the best-known works of English literature in the last century. It tells the story of three children and their mother who are obliged to leave their well-appointed London house and 'play at being poor' in the country when their father is wrongfully arrested. They find a house by the railway line and, from that moment, the railway becomes as much a character in the book as any of the human ones.

In 1972, the Keighley &Worth Valley Railway was the setting for an EMI film of the book, starring Dinah Sheridan, Bernard Cribbins and Jenny Agutter. It became a classic, and the lead actors have been identified by it ever since. Children and their parents are still watching that film today, and still reading the book.

When Carlton TV took the decision to make another film of the book, they were anxious to avoid simply remaking the 1972 film. The idea was to make a grittier, more realistic version, with a dingier and less 'chocolate box' country cottage, grubby pinafores, and trains that looked more 'working clean' than 'just outshopped'. They also wanted a different railway. Several heritage railways were considered, and the Bluebell was eventually chosen, for several reasons. Nesbit herself lived in Kent, and the most likely setting for her imaginary railway was the south-east of England. The Bluebell, by then, in 1999, could boast the all-important (to the plot) tunnel, suitable stations, and locos and rolling stock for the period. The location team were also impressed by the enthusiasm of Operating Manager Chris Knibbs and his colleagues, who went out of their way to show them around and provide what was required.

Before shooting could start, weeks of preparation were necessary. Steps were cut up the embankment at either end of the tunnel, to enable the children to climb easily up and down. Along a stretch of the line through Rock Cutting, the existing fence was replaced by a wooden one for the children to wave to the 'Green Dragon' (C Class No. 592).

For Peter's coal-stealing scene, a large heap was built using 50 tons of coal at the bottom of the bank from the cottages at Horsted Keynes, with a white line painted around the top. Horsted Keynes itself became Mortonhurst for the duration, confusing some of the weekend passengers. Mortonhurst is an entirely fictitious station, as the name of Nesbit's station was never specified in the book.

The landslide was the most difficult and complicated part of the set to construct, and intended to look rather more realistic than the 1972 version. A little way south of Three Arch Bridge, on the steepest side of the bank, an arrangement built on similar lines to a funicular railway was laid down, covered by turf, with trees supported on top of it. At the bottom a row of sleepers was laid, some hinged to collapse over the line when the landslide hit them, spilling earth and stones over the track. The trees were to be lowered from the top of the bank by a tractor to which they were attached by wire, smashing into the sleeper barrier in their descent.

Shooting began early in October 1999, and the first important scene to be filmed was the paper chase scene in and around the tunnel. The hare and hounds enter the tunnel at the north end, shouted at by a group of gangers working nearby – all played by Bluebell volunteers. All hounds but one (Jim) emerge from the south end of the tunnel, and the train that the children had named the 'Green Dragon' hurtles through, emitting what the film unit were pleased to call 'special effects' from the chimney. The children have entered the tunnel to look for the missing hound and cower in a workman's refuge as the train passes – as did the film crew!

One scene in the book that was omitted from the 1972 film was Bobbie's accidental footplate ride. She goes down to the station to ask the driver of the 'Green Dragon' if he could mend Peter's toy engine and, in trying to attract the attention of the crew, falls onto the footplate as the train moves off. There were quite a few problems in filming this scene initially, as the cameraman was unable to get a good view of Bobbie. Eventually, scaffolding was erected on the tender to allow a more elevated angle.

The coal-stealing scene, which occurs early on in the story, was filmed during one chilly night at Horsted. *Maude*, the 0-6-0 tender engine from the Bo'ness & Kinneil Railway, figured large in this scene, hauling a night goods through the station, looking suitably non-pristine and work-weary. As the train passes, Peter creeps behind it towards the coal heap with his wooden trolley. It was some way into the filming before the scene of the children's first visit to the railway was shot. The three children run down the bank from the cottages and across the track to the platform, with the exuberance and enthusiasm of children coming upon a railway for the first time.

Soon after this initial visit to the station, the tear-jerking final scene was filmed. Feeling restless one day during lessons at home, Bobbie goes down to the station, and is greeted in the forecourt by local people waving newspapers and congratulating her. As the train draws in, a figure emerges from the clouds of steam that surround it – 'Oh my Daddy, my Daddy!' – played by Michael Kitchen. One would need to have a heart of stone to remain dry-eyed during the final scene of *The Railway Children*.

The most dramatic moment of the filming was, inevitably, the landslide at Three Arch Bridge, where three weeks' work was destroyed in ten seconds. It was the most tense, nervous moment of the whole shoot, as everyone and everything stood in readiness for the call of 'Turnover … Action!'

There was no going back then. The well-known petticoat scene took place the next day. The children see the landslide and realise that the 11.29 Down will be along before they can get down to the station and warn anyone.

The girls are wearing their red woollen winter petticoats and remove them in order to make flags with which to stop the train and prevent a terrible accident. *Maude* hauled the doomed passenger train and Bobbie was filmed running along towards it in the centre of the running track, veering off at the last minute as the train slides to a halt, and fainting beside the track.

During the final day's filming at the railway, the children were presented with gold watches, a thank-you gift from the grateful railway company for their bravery. This took place on the platforms at Horsted and was followed by scenes with the Old Gentleman (Richard Attenborough) in the waiting room.

It was well known early on that Jenny Agutter would be playing the part of the children's mother, and, although she was hardly required on set at the Bluebell at all, she was present on the final day's filming for a still photo shoot and some newspaper interviews in the *Daily Telegraph*, *Daily Mail*, *OK* magazine, and *What's On TV* magazine.

The film was shown on ITV during the Easter bank holiday of 2000, but the publicity started much earlier than that. Passenger figures were significantly higher the week after filming finished and just after the newspapers had been published, with several people asking if this was the railway where the new *Railway Children* was filmed. One woman went into the shop at Sheffield Park and asked for a *Railway Children* video. When she was presented with the 1972 version she said, 'Oh no, not that one – I want the new one, that was filmed here.' The shop manager had to politely explain that this was not possible; they hadn't actually finished making it yet ...

Mum (Jenny Agutter), the Old Gentleman (Richard Attenborough) and the 'Railway Children', Peter (Jack Blumenau), Phyllis (Clare Thomas) and Roberta 'Bobbie' (Jemima Rooper). (Carlton TV)

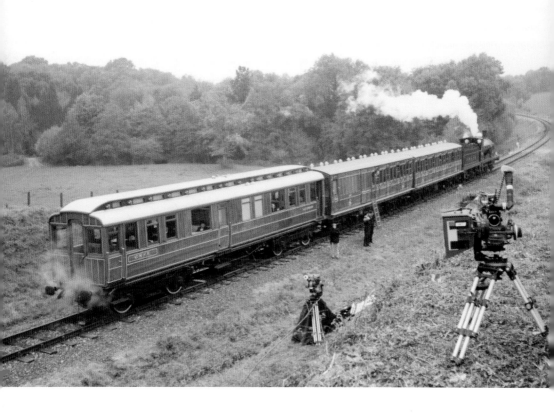

*Above*: The 'Old Gentleman's train' during a break in filming.

*Left*: Porter Perks was played by Gregor Fisher, better known for his string-vested Glaswegian character Rab C. Nesbitt.

*Right*: Jenny Agutter poses at the publicity shoot. (Carlton TV)

*Below*: Red petticoats: stopping the train from hitting the landslide.

# 11

# The 1990s: Television

## Worthy Men and Murderers

The 1990s gave us several TV serials telling the autobiographical stories of characters from times past, including the Irish politician Parnell, Lawrence of Arabia, a Second World War pilot and a notorious murderer. There were fewer adaptations from works of literature than in previous decades, with the notable exception of Hercule Poirot, Agatha Christie's Belgian detective, who never seemed to be away from the Bluebell in the 1990s.

With the fiftieth anniversary of the end of the Second World War in 1995, the 1940s were a popular setting. The Bluebell played its part in the BBC ghost story *Blood and Water*, which tells the story of two friends, Peter and Alex, who meet on a train returning from the Dieppe landings in 1942. The usually familiar surroundings of Sheffield Park and Horsted Keynes may not have been recognisable in the finished film; inside the engine shed at Sheffield Park the buffet car was turned into a hospital van, and at Horsted Keynes the booking hall became an Anderson shelter and the waiting room became the station buffet.

It was the Second World War again in 1996 when Jerome Flynn and Julia Sawalha were at the railway filming *Ain't Misbehavin'*, a comedy drama for ITV, with scenes filmed at Sheffield Park and on the train between Sheffield Park and Horsted Keynes. The train was hauled by No. 73082 *Camelot*, working on its first film job for Bluebell.

Further back in history, in 1992 the BBC made *The Murder of Irene Wilkens*, the re-enactment of a murder that took place in 1921. Horsted Keynes became Bournemouth Central for overnight filming, which took place in January, when the weather played into the hands of the director by being cold and foggy. As the train, hauled by the Q Class No. 541, draws in to the station, the head of Irene Wilkens appears at a carriage window to exchange a few words with a porter amid the swirling dark mist. Unfortunately, the vintage police car that had been hired from Beaulieu to attend the crime scene couldn't make it over the wet, muddy field, so the spare wheel was rolled to the spot in parallel lines to create the impression of the car having been there.

In 1990, Nigel Havers was at the railway in the lead role of LWT's *A Perfect Hero*. Hugh Fleming was a pilot shot down in the Battle of Britain and severely burned, and the series followed his painful and difficult journey back to recovery, including a stay in the renowned Burns Unit at East Grinstead's Queen Victoria Hospital. There he became a member of the famous Guinea Pig Club, formed of airmen undergoing the experimental skin grafting plastic surgery of the surgeon, McIndoe. Bernard Hepton played Hugh's father and James Fox McIndoe, who remodelled his face. Nigel Havers spent much of the series in an uncomfortable latex mask that impaired his vision and took a long time to get on and off each day. Ironically, the train in the scenes shot at the Bluebell wasn't going to East Grinstead but to Norfolk, where Hugh's family lived. He boarded the train at Horsted Keynes and alighted at Sheffield Park to meet his father, with a few scenes filmed in the train on the way. As these scenes took place before Hugh was shot down, Nigel Havers was able to enjoy the experience without being hampered by his 'face'.

Bernard Hepton was back in 1993 in LWT's *Dandelion Dead*. Michael Kitchen played the part of solicitor Major Herbert Armstrong, who keeps arsenic in his garden shed, ostensibly to kill dandelions, but in fact he was attempting to murder his wife, played by Sarah Miles. He administers arsenic in small doses over a period of time, but initially only succeeds in causing her insanity and physical disability. His further attempts finally result in her death, apparently a natural one. However, rival solicitor Oswald Martin (David Thewlis) has his suspicions. Oswald Martin is a self-made man who feels a natural resentment against the sense of entitlement of the officer class (Martin was injured in the trenches) and has no

*Above left*: Julia Sawalha and Jerome Flynn between scenes for ITV's *Ain't Misbehavin'*.

*Above right*: Nigel Havers at the filming of *A Perfect Hero* in 1990.

qualms about bringing Armstrong down. As he coldly points out in an interview with the major, 'We didn't all spend the war playing cricket at Aldershot.'

Filming took place at Sheffield Park, where Bernard Hepton, a colleague of Armstrong's, boarded a train hauled by U Class No. 1618 at Hay station, from which it made several departures.

P. G. Wodehouse's *Jeeves and Wooster* are two of those characters from literature (along with Holmes and Watson, Poirot and Miss Marple) who have been portrayed by a succession of actors over the years. In the early 1990s, LWT made twenty-three episodes of *Jeeves and Wooster*, starring Stephen Fry as Jeeves and Hugh Laurie as Bertie Wooster, an impeccable pairing who managed to capture the characters perfectly. Horsted Keynes featured in episodes 1 and 5, both filmed on the same day. In Episode 1, Horsted Keynes was Westcombe-on-Sea, the Cornish seaside town whither Wooster had been urgently summoned by telegram at the behest of the formidable Aunt Agatha. Jeeves and Wooster arrive on a train hauled by the U Class No. 1618, where they walk along the platform in the company of Horsted Keynes stationmaster Simon Baker, demoted to porter for the occasion and struggling along with their many items of luggage. When Horsted Keynes

Bernard Hepton (right) at Sheffield Park with Bluebell volunteer 'extra' David Harp while filming *Dandelion Dead* for LWT.

changed from Westcombe-on-Sea to Chuffnell Regis, Bertie emerged from the booking hall with a young lady, Pauline, to be met in the forecourt by Jeeves with the car. The forecourt also provided parking for an Aston Martin, an Austin Ascot and an Austin taxi, which set the background as Jeeves, Wooster and Pauline drove away to the country seat of Lord Chuffnell ('Chuffy' when he and Bertie were at school together).

Bertie manages to get into hot water with Pauline, to the annoyance of her jealous boyfriend, and ends up doing a moonlight flit, on his own, back to the station. During the night shoot, the booking clerk is alone in his office, lit by the yellow glow of the lamp, with his kettle steaming on the hob. Needless to say, whatever Bertie's latest hare-brained scheme is, he doesn't get away with it, and ends up having to be extricated from his difficulties by Jeeves as usual.

In what became a six-hour mini-series, Ralph Fiennes came to Horsted Keynes in 1990 to star in *A Dangerous Man: Lawrence after Arabia*, a biographical drama based on actual events. It depicts famed British military officer and liaison T. E. Lawrence (Fiennes) as he accompanies Arab leader Emir Feisal (Siddig El Fadil) to the 1919 peace conference in Paris. Lawrence, determined to support Arab independence, proves to be an extremely popular figure, but France and England remain wary about Feisal's request for autonomy. Lawrence's fame eventually makes Feisal grow resentful of him, taking its toll on their close partnership.

Jeeves and Wooster (Stephen Fry and Hugh Laurie) arrive at Westcombe-on-Sea (Horsted Keynes) to visit formidable Aunt Agatha, accompanied by stationmaster Simon Baker, demoted in this instance to porter to struggle with their luggage.

Ralph Fiennes rests between takes as Lawrence of Arabia in *A Dangerous Man*.

## The Little Belgian Detective

David Suchet was asked to play Agatha Christie's Hercule Poirot in 1988, and, after the success of that first series, the germ of an idea began to dawn. How would it be, he thought, if he could play Poirot in every story about him that Christie had written – seventy short stories and novels in all. There were times, after some of the series, when LWT almost decided to call it a day, but in the end they did make all the stories, and David Suchet went on to play the detective in his last case, *Curtain*, in 2012, twenty-four years after first portraying him.

Poirot, rather like that other fictional detective Sherlock Holmes, travelled all over the country solving cases by train, and passed through Horsted Keynes on many occasions. In June 1990 the station became Styles St Mary in 1920, the setting for the first of the Poirot novels, *The Mysterious Affair at Styles*. By then, several of the Poirot short stories had already been filmed, so this two-hour special was a bit of a journey back in time for the characters, who were usually seen to inhabit the 1930s. This special had been timed to coincide with the centenary of Agatha Christie's birth in 1890, which was celebrated on the screen in September 1990.

Captain Hastings has been invalided home from the front and goes to spend his sick leave at Styles Court, the home of an old friend, John Cavendish, now the local squire. He arrives at Styles St Mary (Horsted Keynes) in a train hauled by the Adams tank No. 488,

David Suchet (Hercule Poirot) never seemed to be away from the Bluebell in the 1990s.

pulling in with its drain cocks open, a common request of directors. He walks out through the booking hall and out to the forecourt, where he is met by Cavendish with his car. He informs Hastings that he can 'still get a drop of petrol – thanks to the Ministry of Agriculture'. They then drive off along the road to the field, looking suitably rural and passing a bicycle and another car as they disappear into the next shot – another road entirely.

During two very hot days in July 1990 the LWT crew was back at the railway filming for two short stories, *The Double Clue* and *The Plymouth Express*. Agatha Christie wrote several stories set on trains – a useful ruse as all the suspects were captive for the duration of the journey. *The Double Clue* was one of Christie's less meaty short stories, which LWT padded out with a long drawn-out dalliance between Poirot and the Countess Rossakoff.

In *The Plymouth Express*, another short story, Poirot is presented with the body of a woman discovered under the seat of a railway carriage, her jewels missing; a storyline that she developed further in her full-length novel *The Blue Train*. Schools Class loco No. 928

*Stowe* was renumbered 777 for the filming, hauling a six-coach train along the length of the line.

During filming on the train, a suspicious-looking man in an overcoat, carrying a newspaper, passes along the corridor and enters the compartment of the heroine, Florence, who occupies it alone. She fails to change trains as planned at Bristol, telling her maid that she had 'business further down the line' and will meet her later, and rouses suspicions when she fails to do so. Two men board the train at Plymouth and find Florence's body under the seat in their compartment. Poirot and Captain Hastings decide to recreate the fateful journey, travelling along the line from Sheffield Park to West Hoathly, in a Pullman car, Poirot carefully timing the station stops as they proceed. At Horsted Keynes (Weston) they alight and interview the paper boy on the platform, amid a bustle of passengers, about a lady in a blue coat and hat who got off and bought a paper yesterday at precisely

David Suchet (Poirot) with his trusted sidekick Captain Hastings at the railway for *The Plymouth Express*.

this time. In the denouement, a flashback shows Florence being stabbed and dragging her bloody hands down the carriage window in a most dramatic fashion.

*The ABC Murders*, written in 1936, was one of Agatha Christie's best-known novels. Hercule Poirot receives a series of letters warning him that a murder is shortly to take place, and where – and they all do. Mrs Ascher at Andover, Betty Barnard at Bexhill, and Carmichael Clarke at Churston. Beside each body is a copy of the *ABC Railway Guide*. Poirot is determined that the proposed murder at Doncaster will not take place.

In May 1991, Horsted Keynes station stood in for various destinations in *The ABC Murders* during two very long days of filming, with David Suchet as Poirot, Hugh Fraser as Captain Hastings, Philip Jackson as Inspector Japp and Donald Sumpter as Alexander Bonaparte Cust, the chief suspect.

The U Class No. 1618 worked as hard as the Schools Class had the previous summer, in steam for over twenty hours each day as it busied itself hauling trains from London Victoria to Andover, Bexhill, Churston and Doncaster, and between Sheffield Park and Horsted Keynes about ten times for passing shots – even though it was pointed out to the directors that the line to Bexhill had been electrified in the 1930s, this mattered not; it had to be 'steam' of course.

*Dead Man's Mirror*, written in 1937, was one of Christie's less remarkable 'locked room mystery' short stories. Filming at Horsted Keynes station in 1992 made the most of the location, as scenes were shot in the train, on the platforms, and in the forecourt. A bustling platform represented, as so often before, London Victoria, and the forecourt stood in as the branch-line station of Whimperley.

Poirot and Hastings alight from an Austin 10 at Whimperley station for *Dead Man's Mirror*.

# 12

# The 2000s

## The New Millennium

This was a time when film making and viewing were changing with unprecedented rapidity. With the arrival of Netflix, Blu-ray and 'watch again' facilities, options were wider than they had ever been, and we were moving towards more virtual films and serials – box sets without the actual boxes. The equipment brought on location is lighter and smaller than ever, requiring less power – and often with the background added later on blue screen and a drone for the overhead shots.

The Bluebell was still appearing frequently on television and cinema screens and, with the popularity of 'reality' television, appearing more often as itself, in programmes such as *Scrapheap Challenge*. Hercule Poirot and Miss Marple were still around, in the company of other figures from the literature of previous centuries, such as *Uncle Silas* and *Tess of the d'Urbervilles*. *Downton Abbey* made its appearance on our screens, with Horsted Keynes becoming Downton station through several series. The railway also appeared in some notable films of the time, *Sherlock*, *Charlotte* and *Miss Potter*, and dipped its toe into the waters of horror and Muppetry.

## TV Adverts

By the new millennium, the number of adverts was beginning to thin out a bit, but there was still a wide variety of products and services using the Bluebell as a sales pitch. Products as diverse as a three-piece suite, McCain oven chips and Panasonic cameras were advertised here and, most entertainingly, VI sprung beds. For this advert, a 1930s scene was set up at Sheffield Park, including the Orient Express about to leave for Venice. An elegant couple is about to join the train, along with their VI sprung bed, without which the lady refuses to travel. The black and white photograph appeared in a number of Sunday magazines, with the entire image transposed in one of them, the wording on the station signs and the Pullman lettering all the wrong way round.

An entire day in 2003 was spent filming 'a leaf falling onto a railway line' for McCain oven chips. Perhaps they were special 'lite' chips. The 'leaves on the line' theme was repeated in 2006 in an advert for broadband, which allowed you to watch your favourite programmes whatever time you got home – leaves on the line notwithstanding. On a pleasant, balmy day in October, a crew of around twenty descended on Leamland Bridge at Horsted Keynes to film a leaf falling onto a railway line. It took them all day, and they even brought their own sycamore leaves with them.

## Television

New channels and new technology were burgeoning as the new millennium dawned, and the railway provided the background to promote them. The new (to the UK) Discovery Channel was dedicated to education and information, intended to be of interest to those parents who wanted their children to gain something from the hours spent in front of the box, and those who wanted to improve their own knowledge.

The Bluebell turned up on this channel, and on the traditional ones, largely as an attractive backdrop, but also in a more prominent role in *Scrapheap Challenge*.

Readers who have no children or grandchildren may not be familiar with *The Tweenies*. These were life-size, brightly coloured and garishly dressed characters whose remit was to entertain and inform the very young on television in the mornings. *The Tweenies* attended a small and very select playgroup, where they sang songs, listened to stories and learned about the world. They were all at the railway in December 2001, learning all about 'Going Underground'. Underground was supplied by our own tunnel.

Youngsters were at the fore again for a rather gimmicky programme on Channel 5 about the things that fathers and sons do together. The pair chosen for the programme

Ex-*Grange Hill* and *Eastenders* star Todd Carty and his son, James, learn how to handle a steam engine together for a Channel 5 programme about fathers and sons doing things together.

were former *Eastenders* actor Todd Carty and his young son James, neither of whom had volunteered on a railway before. Todd and James had landed the task of learning to handle a steam engine and came to Sheffield Park for some tuition from ex-Nine Elms driver Clive Groome. They were instructed in the basic principles of the steam engine and had a go at lighting up and oiling round, and learned such valuable skills as cutting cloth with a spanner and throwing out a fire.

## Scrapheap Challenge

Channel 4's *Scrapheap Challenge* was the precursor to many of the competitive reality programmes that issue some kind of task to be performed against the clock that are still popular today. Two teams were pitted against each other to build some kind of device to perform an allotted task, with ten hours to build it before having to demonstrate its fitness (or otherwise) for purpose. The winning team was the one that completed the task in the shortest time, provided that their machine fulfilled the criteria.

Each team had four members; one technical consultant who had some foreknowledge of the project and could do a bit of forward thinking, and three other members who were completely in the dark until a few minutes before the sounding of the starting gong. Each team was provided with a work station equipped with welding and cutting facilities and basic tools, the two areas screened off from each other. The whole thing was set in a large scrapyard and the teams expected to use whatever could be found there. Two presenters were on the set, and made it their job to wander in and out of the work areas expressing incredulity and doubt with an air of undisguised pessimism.

Each programme also had an expert in the field of the particular device being built who explained the technology to the viewer and adjudicated on whether the set task has been achieved. Mobile cranes, power boats, submarines and a tunnel boring machine had been produced by the time that Channel 4 approached the Bluebell about making a road/rail vehicle, and filming started in April 2002. The Bluebell provided railway expert Norman Blake and technical consultant Tony Deller. The set task was to build a road/rail vehicle that could be driven on the road up to the railway line, placed on the tracks, negotiate points, haul a modest load up a slight gradient and stop at a predetermined point. The vehicle to complete all these tests in the shortest time was the winner.

The Tunnel Ratz team was made up of three London Underground rolling-stock fitters, one of whom was a keen motorcyclist, so their vehicle was based around a motorbike. The Pit Stop Crew were a Formula One pit crew, who converted a black cab.

Teams and film crew turned up at the secret scrapheap location at 6 a.m., and the teams were set onto the task at 7 a.m. The Pit Stop Crew soon found a taxi behind a bus (which had to be moved) and the Tunnel Ratz had to choose one of the number of motorcycles that was powerful enough, and working.

The Pit Stop Crew found that the taxi wheels fitted the railway gauge, and made some rail wheels out of brake discs and steel tube, and devised an arrangement for raising and lowering them as required. The Tunnel Ratz took a long time getting started, and seemed to waste time getting their chosen motorbike to work. They fashioned a sidecar to balance on the rails, and made their rail wheels from car wheels with their tyres removed. On the rails, the front rail wheels held the front bike wheel clear of the railway line as though the bike were doing a perpetual wheelie.

Popular opinion favoured the taxi during the construction, as the motorbike had no reverse gear and had to be lifted off the line and turned around at the end, which made it look like a long shot at the time. Construction went on until late in the evening, and, of course, there was a last-minute panic, but, just in time, the vehicles were finished and the race was on.

The vehicles were to be tested at Horsted Keynes station, and the idea had been to race them side by side through the station. However, the dangers posed by a possible derailment were such that the decision was made to run the vehicles over the same course and time each one. The vehicles and film crews arrived early on the day of filming to cold wind and heavy rain – it was April after all. The morning was spent setting up camera positions, walking the route and giving safety briefings. The vehicles were brought down to the carriage yard, and the teams were allowed one final hour for last-minute tinkering and adjustments.

Fortunately, the afternoon of the race was fine with some sun. The vehicles were first driven to the crossing near the signal box, where they had to convert to rail mode and drive through the station via Platform 2 to the starter signal at the end. There, a platelayer's Wickham trolley was attached and had to be hauled as far as Leamland Bridge. The Wickham was uncoupled here, as there were understandable concerns about the braking down the gradient back into the station, so the vehicles had to run back through the platform and stop exactly at a milk churn placed alongside the 9F loco No. 92240, which had been included for colour, and to provide the 'starting whistle'.

It was a close-run thing in the final stages – the taxi seemed to be at an advantage, being less unwieldy and seemingly more stable, but, on the final run, it derailed just outside the railway cottages, putting itself out of the running, and the crown went to the Tunnel Ratz with their motorbike.

*Scrapheap Challenge* runners-up with their car-based road/railer machine, which derailed just before the finishing line.

# TV Serials

The Bluebell appeared in a number of TV serials during the early years of the twenty-first century – many of them based on works of literature from the Victorian era to the 1950s, pretty much covering the age of steam.

Biographies were popular, telling the life stories of such political heavyweights as Churchill and Alan Clark and the scientists Einstein and Eddington. Fictional sleuths Hercule Poirot and Miss Marple were still around and were joined by Inspector Foyle, played by Michael Kitchen. There was also a new trend in crime drama, with two dramatisations of real-life Victorian murders. Early on in the decade, Gemma Arterton and Eddie Redmayne started their careers in *Tess of the d'Urbervilles* and *Downton Abbey* appeared on our screens on a Sunday evening.

The ever-versatile Horsted Keynes left its Victorian heritage behind in the spring of 2001 when it set the scene for a TV adaptation of Kingsley Amis' novel *Lucky Jim*, set in the 1950s. The Jim of the title, Jim Dixon, manages to fall into a lecturing job at one of Britain's new universities (very much looked down upon, both socially and academically, by the 'old' universities) more or less by default. In the first scene at Horsted Keynes, Jim and his girlfriend Christine leave for a new life in London, changing at Luton Town (Horsted) where engine *Camelot* and the Class 4 loco were in and out of the station, making it appear busy.

Horsted Keynes was back to its customary Victorian setting in 2006 for a BBC series based on Phillip Pullman's *The Sally Lockhart Mysteries*. *Ruby in the Smoke* (the smoke having more to do with the London smog than Bluebell's trains) starred Julie Walters as Mrs Holland and Billie Piper as Sally Lockhart. Although it purported to be of the Victorian era, all the dialogue was modern in every respect, using contemporary sentence construction, turns of phrase and slang, so the series had the appearance of a soap opera where all the characters happened, by chance, to be in Victorian dress. As a period drama, it struck a bum note, but Horsted Keynes was very attractive as the quiet Swaleness station, peopled only by one family and a few soldiers as Sally boards the train – followed, unbeknown by her, by Mrs Holland.

In 2006, David Tennant was most famous for his role as the Doctor in the long-running sci-fi drama *Doctor Who*, but he was at the Bluebell in May of that year in a very different character, playing the part of Eddington in *Einstein and Eddington*, set during the First World War. Eddington is employed by the government to prove that Einstein's theories are correct – or not. Taking a break from scientific studies, he cycles to Cambridge station (a role reprised by Horsted Keynes station once again) to see off his gay soldier friend William, leaving for the front. In the general melee and the inevitable emotional maelstrom on the platform, Eddington becomes distracted by a father (Jim Broadbent) seeing off his son to the same grim destination. The upshot of all this is that the train leaves before Eddington has had a chance to say goodbye to William. Undaunted, he sets off at breakneck speed on his bicycle and races the train along an adjacent road (the track beside the line from Horsted Keynes to West Hoathly) so that he can wave goodbye 'properly' to William, whom, of course, he never sees again. The GWR Dukedog engine and the 100-seater carriages were used for this shot, and David Tennant did all his own stunts with the bicycle, which he did have to ride extremely fast – even to keep up with the Dukedog.

*Right*: Sally Lockhart (Billie Piper) and Mrs Holland (Julie Walters) during filming of *Ruby in the Smoke*.

*Below*: Eddington (David Tennant) prepares to 'race the train' on his bicycle in *Einstein and Eddington*.

In 2001 it was the turn of Kingscote station to take centre stage. *My Uncle Silas* was an ITV series based on the short stories of H. E. Bates, set during the turn of the last century, when young Ned spends two long, hot summers staying with his Uncle Silas in the village of Souldrop, learning the ways of the countryside – not all of them quite on the right side of the law. Uncle Silas (Albert Finney) lives with his housekeeper Mrs Betts (Sue Johnston), and they make a pretty pair. Silas has two interests in life, women and home-made wine, and Mrs Betts makes it her business to prevent him from indulging in either.

In 'Queenie White' Mrs Betts packs Silas and Ned off to a painting and decorating job in a hotel, suitably distant for them to have to stay and be out of her way for a few days. It is a temperance hotel, the one place that she can be assured of Silas not falling prey to the temptations of the bar, but he only discovers this as they pull up at Swineshead station (Kingscote) in the pony and trap. The exterior of the hotel is Kingscote station, and the landlord Charles White (Paul Bown) is up a ladder putting up the Temperance Hotel sign over the old Station Hotel sign.

Mr White turns out to be a mean-spirited, miserly, humourless teetotaller, converted to taking the pledge by his sister. He lays out the terms of employment for Silas and Ned, and puts them in the room nearest the railway line, where they can see, out of the window, the C Class noisily passing with a train to the seaside.

'I don't mind,' says Ned, 'I like trains.'

Charles' wife Queenie turns out to be a sunny-natured woman, treated as free labour by her husband, who had taken her from a life of drudgery as a chambermaid to set up a hotel with him – a new life of drudgery, as it turned out. One day, when Charles is out on business, Silas persuades Queenie to go with him for a day out to the seaside; she has never been to the seaside, or even been on a train. They travel first class in a compartment on their own, with shots taken along the lineside and on the footplate, setting the scene with the gleaming brasswork on the boiler backplate and dripping injector, as well as Silas and Queenie letting their hair down in the carriage. After an idyllic, sunny day out at the seaside, they return to the hotel on the same train. The first shot is of the train being propelled – probably an 'extra' shot taken of the stock being propelled back to the station ready for the next shot – but, by the time that the train arrives back at Swineshead, it has miraculously turned around again.

By the time that Silas and Ned are ready to leave Swineshead station, there have been some changes. The Temperance Hotel is the Station Hotel once more, and Queenie has insisted upon Charles employing two extra staff, including a barmaid – yes, a barmaid! The final scene shows Silas and Ned driving out of the garden at Kingscote station, into the forecourt and off up the lane, waving to Queenie as she stands outside the hotel, as the Temperance Hotel sign is taken down for good.

Horsted Keynes station and the adjoining picnic field were back in the limelight in 2007 with a foray into comedy. Two sketches were filmed there for *That Mitchell and Webb Look*, a spin-off of the Radio 4 comedy *The Mitchell and Webb Sound*, starring David Mitchell and Robert Webb. Locomotive *Fenchurch* hauled an Edwardian train for a scene involving a man with TB coughing in one of the compartments, but the other sketch went considerably further back in time to the Roman occupation of Britain, centuries before trains were so much as a twinkle in Stephenson's eye, and this was filmed in the picnic field. A Roman barbeque was built for the scene, and an Irish wolfhound engaged to lick the face of one of the actors. The dog showed a strong disinclination to do this, and the efforts of the film crew to persuade her to do her stuff were much funnier than the actual sketch turned out to be.

The Bluebell was the setting for two political biographies during this decade as Winston Churchill and Alan Clark both came to the small screen. The film *The Gathering Storm*, made in 2001, told the story of the years leading up to the Second World War at the time when Churchill was at the height of his power. Horsted Keynes station at night was the setting for a scene in which Churchill (Albert Finney) alights from the train and tries in vain to communicate with his wife Clemmie (Vanessa Redgrave), who was still inside the carriage and resolutely refusing to acknowledge him as the train pulled away. On this occasion, Horsted Keynes played itself. The director had decided that Churchill, travelling via East Grinstead, would have been highly likely to break his journey at Horsted Keynes to visit Harold MacMillan at his home in Birch Grove, his country seat just up the road from the station.

*Above left*: David Mitchell enjoys a Roman barbeque in the field at Horsted Keynes in *That Mitchell and Webb Look*.

*Above right*: Albert Finney as Winston Churchill at Horsted Keynes.

Alan Clark (John Hurt) and his wife (Jenny Agutter) in the BBC serial *The Alan Clark Diaries*.

In 2003 Kingscote station was back in the billing as the setting for the BBC serial *The Alan Clark Diaries*, telling the story of the life of the MP through his own eyes and pen. Alan Clark (John Hurt) and his wife (Jenny Agutter, last seen at the railway as the mother in *The Railway Children*) arrived at and departed from Kingscote aboard several trains during the day, and finally drove away from the station in his Rolls-Royce – the very one that had belonged to the MP himself.

## Sleuths of Fiction: Poirot, Marple, and Foyle

Having determined to film every Poirot story that Agatha Christie had ever written, David Suchet was still a regular figure at the railway into the twenty-first century. *Curtain*, his last story and the one that depicts the death of the Belgian detective, was screened in 2012. David Suchet made his final visit to Horsted Keynes station in the autumn of 2007 to film *Mrs McGinty's Dead*. He commented, during the shoot, that he had been coming to the station, on and off, for twenty years, as he first visited in 1987 to film *A Mysterious Affair at Styles*.

On that autumn day in 2007 he had moved forward to the 1930s (although *Mrs McGinty's Dead* was actually written and set in 1950) and Horsted was standing in for Broadhinney and Kilchester stations. Broadhinney is the small village where the murder of Mrs McGinty takes place, and Kilchester a much bigger, busier station, where Poirot has a narrow escape. Having made some uncomfortable discoveries about some of the residents of Broadhinney, he is waiting for a train at Kilchester when someone pushes him hard in the small of the

After twenty years on and off of visiting Bluebell, Hercule Poirot (David Suchet) made his final visit in 2007.

back on the platform edge just as the train, hauled by the U Class No. 1638, hurtles past with a non-stop train. He is pulled from the brink of death by an army sergeant in the nick of time and Mrs Rendell is observed hurrying away from the scene ...

Agatha Christie's other sleuth, Miss Marple, has had many incarnations over the years, most notably Margaret Rutherford on film, Joan Hickson, Geraldine McEwan and Julia McKenzie on television, and June Whitfield on the radio. *Murder at the Vicarage* was first published in 1930, but in a version starring Geraldine McEwan it was set in the 1950s with flashbacks to Miss Marple's youth in the First World War, when she lost her fiancé and never married. In 2004 the scenes from the war were filmed at Horsted station, once again doing double duty as the quaint little station in the village of St Mary Mead, Miss Marple's home, and a busy London station where troop trains and hospital trains transporting the wounded are continually arriving and departing. A very young Miss Marple is there, reminded of events during her youth while investigating the death of Colonel Protheroe in the vicar's study.

In 2008, Julie McKenzie played Miss Marple in *Why Didn't They Ask Evans?* set in the early 1930s. Bobby Jones finds a dying man in the dunes of a golf course, whose last words, 'Why didn't they ask Evans?', and a photograph are the only clues to the identity of the murderer. Bobby has two redoubtable ladies to assist him – Lady Frances 'Frankie' Derwent and Miss Marple (Julia McKenzie). Bobby (Sean Biggerstaff) is seen off at Little Standing station (Horsted Keynes) by Miss Marple, to attend the inquest, and meets Frankie (Georgia Moffett) on the train, which is where their collaboration begins.

Miss Marple (Julia McKenzie) during filming of Agatha Christie's *Why Didn't They Ask Evans?*

The series *Foyle's War* featured Detective Inspector Foyle, who was refused a commission during the Second World War because of his age and finds himself stuck in a routine police job with falling crime figures and nothing much to do. Then he gets called to investigate a murder and the job looks like becoming interesting again. Unable to drive, he is assigned a driver from the Mechanised Transport Corps as all the policemen have been called up. Cue the arrival of jolly-hockey-sticks driver Samantha (Sam) Stewart (Honeysuckle Weeks), and an unorthodox partnership is born.

Two episodes of *Foyle's War* featured the Bluebell as the background. One used Horsted Keynes as a setting for the usual arrival and departure of trains, and the other, 'The Russian House', was rather more unusual and used Imberhorne Viaduct, just south of East Grinstead, as the scene of a suicide, before the Bluebell Railway had extended track onto the viaduct.

A lorry taking prisoners of war away from a camp to be repatriated is crossing the viaduct when they attempt to escape out of the back of it. They are forced back by the accompanying soldiers, with the exception of one, who runs to the parapet and jumps over. The stunt man who threw himself off the viaduct did so only once – onto a sort of bouncy castle surrounded by cardboard boxes on the (closed) road below.

# Murder Real and Imagined

Two series were made at around the same time depicting real life, and very bloody murders committed in the 1860s. They related the efforts of the detectives who attempted to track down the killers in the days before DNA testing and forensic medicine, and before detection was an accepted profession.

*The Suspicions of Mr Whicher* was based on the book by Kate Summerscale about the particularly grisly murder of three-year-old Saville Kent at Road Hill House in Wiltshire, who was found one morning in 1860 pushed down the outside privy with his throat cut and his head almost severed from his neck. The detective, Mr Whicher (Paddy Considine), suspected Saville's sixteen-year-old sister Constance of the crime, but was unable to prove it. In October 2010, *Fenchurch* and the vintage carriage set were used to convey Mr Whicher from the bustling metropolis to the sleepy Wiltshire village where the murder took place, to begin his tireless investigation.

The first recorded railway murder, of Thomas Briggs, took place on 9 July 1864 on the North London Railway. The story is based on a true account laid down in the book *Mr Briggs' Hat* by Kate Colquhoun and starts with the grisly discovery made by two bank clerks boarding the train at Hackney one summer evening. They sat down, felt a damp sensation in their nether regions, and got up to see their hands and trousers stained with fresh blood. The cushions were soaked with it, and further investigation revealed the walls and door of the carriage were also liberally smeared with gore. The opening scene of the story introduces the narrator, who buys a songsheet from a ballad boy outside Hackney Central station, singing the story of the murder; Horsted Keynes becomes Hackney Central on this occasion.

The film crew spent a cold night outside the cottages at Horsted Keynes, filming the finding of the body, and a day in the running shed, inside an LB&SCR first-class carriage. After the clerks had discovered the murder scene, the guard locked the compartment and the train continued to its terminus at Chalk Farm, where it was met by the line superintendent, who had been alerted by telegraph. Then, and only then, were the police called to the scene. Inside the carriage, Inspector Tanner describes the murder scene as it was originally found, with the intriguing clues of a heavy knobbed stick, black bag, and a crumpled hat not belonging to Mr Briggs.

## Tess of the d'Urbervilles

Thomas Hardy's bucolic tragedy *Tess of the d'Urbervilles* has spawned several film and TV adaptations, and in 2008 the BBC made a new version of the story, in an attempt to shed the chocolate-box, Constable-painting-type image of Hardy's Wessex and aim for a more realistic interpretation.

Dairymaid Tess, as a very young woman, has an illegitimate child as the result of a rape by a 'gentleman', Alec d'Urberville, the child dying in babyhood. Time passes and she marries dairyman Angel Clare; divulging her past secret to him on their wedding night, he then rejects her and she has to leave him and work the land in poverty and hardship. In this adaptation, the mud, drudgery and exhaustion of poorly paid female farm labourers were uncompromisingly portrayed.

During the filming, Horsted Keynes became Sandbourne station for one day and the Vale of Great Dairies on the next day. For the first shot, Sandbourne was a busy station, with *Fenchurch* and the 01 Class locomotives in and out of various platforms with their trains, and Angel Clare awaits the train that will take him to his new job as dairyman in the dairy where he will meet Tess. The scene at the Vale of Great Dairies took place in torrential rain (provided by the film unit) at a time in the story when Angel and Tess were falling for each other. A wagon is drawn up alongside the platform, and Angel and a station porter are loading milk churns in the downpour, watched from the shelter of the canopy by Tess, 'sick with love'.

The second scene filmed at Sandbourne occurred towards the tragic end of the story. Tess has been taken out of abject poverty to live with the father of her child, Alec d'Urberville, as his mistress, subject to his every whim and in his vindictive power. In one of his most chilling scenes, Hardy coolly describes their landlady investigating something dripping through her ceiling – the blood of d'Urberville, murdered by Tess. She has long since fled the scene, and, reunited with Angel, they both desperately attempt to escape retribution. They leave the train at Sandbourne and run along the railway line in the northern direction in what ends up being a futile attempt to flee from the police.

This BBC series was the springboard to a glittering career for both Gemma Arterton (Tess) and Eddie Redmayne (Angel Clare). Gemma Arterton took the lead in the remake of *St Trinians* and Eddie Redmayne won an Oscar for his performance as Steven Hawking in *The Theory of Everything*.

Eddie Redmayne (Angel) and Gemma Arterton (Tess) at Horsted Keynes for *Tess of the D'Urbervilles*.

## North & South

Written by Elizabeth Gaskell and published in 1854, *North & South* is a story of the north/south and gentility/self-made man divide. Margaret has been brought up in a Devonshire parsonage, but is forced to leave it for the industrial town of Milton (Manchester) when her father defects from the Church after losing his faith. There she becomes involved with influential mill owner John Thornton and embroiled in strikes, industrial unrest, and all sorts of unladylike goings-on.

Three scenes from the book were filmed at Horsted Keynes and on the train down the line. Of course, the engine presented something of a problem, as the railway couldn't supply one built before 1854, so they made do with the Dukedog and the 01, keeping them a little hazy and out of shot as much as possible.

The first scene was the protracted move from Devonshire to Milton. Margaret Hale (Daniela Denby-Ashe), her mother Maria (Lesley Manville) and father (Tim Pigott-Smith) undertake the journey with Dixon the faithful maid (Pauline Quirke) fussing around generally. It is a sad time, leaving behind all that they loved, and tears are shed in the carriage once they are on the way.

The second scene takes place much later in the story, shortly before the death of Mrs Hale, and involves her son Frederick (Rupert Evans). Accused of mutiny in the navy and banished from the country until he can clear his name, he risks capture and death to come to England and see his mother before she dies. Afterwards, his sister Margaret secretly conveys him to the station at night to catch the last train to London and return to Spain. She is spotted by Thornton (Richard Armitage) fondly embracing an unknown man at the station, unchaperoned and late at night, and he draws the inevitable conclusions. At the last minute, Frederick is recognised by a local man, Leonards (Russell Mabey), a member of the station staff. A scuffle ensues, and Leonards is pushed onto the track by Frederick, who makes his escape on the train.

'A door was opened in a carriage, he jumped in, and he leant out to say: "God bless you Margaret", the train rushed past her, and she was left standing alone. She was so terribly sick and faint that she was thankful to be able to turn into the ladies' waiting room and sit down for an instant.'

Leonards appears to have walked away unhurt, but dies later. Was it down to the injuries that he received or just his habitual heavy drinking? The scene was filmed on the island platform, and Leonards, in a suitably padded costume, was thrown down the subway steps before Frederick caught his train. Later, Margaret was filmed catching her own train back into Milton, very fearful all the time that a member of the station staff could turn out to be Leonards and recognise her as Frederick's companion.

The last scene to be filmed was also at night, a scene mentioned but not described in the book. Wages in Thornton's mill are lowered to compete with cut-price imported American yarns; the hands go on strike, and Thornton brings in new cheap labour from Ireland.

'Can't you get hands from Ireland? I wouldn't keep these fellows a day, I'd teach them that I was master, and could employ what servants I liked.'

'Yes, to be sure I can, and will, too, if they go on long. It will be trouble and expense, and I fear some danger, but I will do it, rather than give in.'

A rake of trucks was placed in the siding under the cottages at Horsted, and doused with water by the volunteers of the Bluebell fire service to give the appearance of a dank, foggy Midlands

Margaret Hale (Daniela Denby-Ashe), her mother Maria (Lesley Manville), and father (Tim Pigott-Smith) relax before undertaking a train journey with Dixon, their faithful maid (Pauline Quirke).

evening when furtive, dark deeds are afoot. Smoke guns added to the atmosphere (actually it was a warm, pleasant June night) and the arc lights eerily pierced the gloom. The Irish mill workers who have arrived in the trucks – men, women and some children – climb down out of the train and are escorted stealthily away in the direction of the mill. It all ends in a riot, of course.

## The Downton Chronicles

*Downton Abbey* quickly became the runaway Sunday night TV success of the early 2000s. It was shown around the world and was particularly popular in America, where Downton tea parties became all the rage. When our daughter Clarrie was in Detroit she was asked whether life in England is really like *Downton Abbey*. She decided against trying to explain that for her parents it kind of is because they live at Downton station, and went with a straightforward 'no'.

The series opens in April 1912 with a message being sent via the telegraph. In the opening sequence, a mixed train, hauled by a 'Terrier' locomotive, is steaming through the Kent marshes very early on a spring morning, the new valet Mr Bates travelling in the milk train to take up his new position at Downton Abbey. The camera moves away from the train to the telegraph wires strung between the poles, passing in their endless sequence as the journey progresses. It then follows a single telegraph wire along a village street to a post office, the destination of the telegraph message. The *Titanic* has been hit by an iceberg and sunk, with the loss of many lives – including the heir to the title Earl of Grantham and the Downton estate; news that changes everything in that great house.

That opening sequence was filmed at the Kent & East Sussex Railway, the only railway in the country that still has over 10 miles of working telegraph lines, but for the series Horsted Keynes became Downton station, situated in the village of Downton. It was originally called Downton Village, but became simply Downton after the first time. It was the scene of many meetings and partings over the ensuing years as the characters arrived and departed, not always in perfect harmony.

There was a great deal of subterfuge over Marigold, the illegitimate daughter of Lady Edith, who was brought up on one of the farms on the estate until Lady Edith took her to live at the house as her 'ward'. To begin with, nobody but Lady Edith's aunt knew about Marigold, but once Lady Grantham (Lady Edith's mother) found out the truth a scheme was planned to hand the little girl over from the farmer to Lady Edith at the station, which is scuppered when Lady Mary (Edith's sister) and her maid appear at the station – and they are not in on the secret.

The most famous of the railway scenes occurs in the second series and depicts Matthew Crawley, the new heir to Downton, departing for the front to be seen off by Lady Mary. Although they marry later on, at this time in the series they have broken off an 'understanding' (they were never quite engaged) and Matthew is engaged to Lavinia Swire.

The runaway Sunday night TV success of the early 2000s was *Downton Abbey* and Bluebell played its railway scenes through several eras. Lady Edith, Lady Mary and Matthew Crawley are at Downton station.

*Above*: Maggie Smith (Dowager Duchess) and Samantha Bond (Lady Rosamund Painswick).

*Left*: Michelle Dockery (Lady Mary) and Dan Stevens (Matthew Crawley).

Maggie Smith (Dowager Duchess), Penelope Wilton (Mrs Isobel Crawley) and Elizabeth McGovern (Lady Grantham).

The parting was restrained but heavy with hidden meaning; Lady Mary gives Matthew her lucky mascot, an old toy dog, before he boards the train and disappears to almost certain death. In interviews, Michelle Dockery (Lady Mary) admits that Horsted Keynes station has a special place in her heart because of some of her scenes there – seeing Matthew off to war, accepting a 'good match' proposal from Sir Richard Carlisle, and going into labour as she steps off the train after a long journey back from Scotland. Producer Gareth Neame, writer Julian Fellowes, and composer John Lunn also agree that the 'Matthew off to war' scene was one of the most important in the series.

# 13

# The 2000s: Films

## Wrecked Trains, Horror, and Muppetry

Films made at the Bluebell have never been short on variety, and the new millennium was no exception. There was a spate of Second World War-based dramas, one or two modern-day productions, one train crash and three trains blown up.

Horsted Keynes station dipped its toe in the water of the Hammer Horror genre with *The Woman in Black* and its sequel *Angel of Death*, and provided the background for the latest Muppet movie.

Not all requirements for a location were quite so dramatic or high profile as these. *Creatures*, set-in modern-day Glasgow, was part mystery, part romance, similar to *Trainspotting*, but not quite so grim. During their day at the Bluebell, the crew filmed (seemingly interminably) a golf ball landing on the bonnet of a car with a policeman standing beside it, track passing beneath the train, and carriages passing under the footbridge at Sheffield Park. The 9F No. 92240 performed the necessary duties, but was kept out of shot and only used during the title sequence.

Cruella Productions (an offshoot of Disney) spent a long, cold night in December 1999 in Horsted Keynes signal box filming for family comedy film *102 Dalmatians*. The signal box was renamed Green Park and became a temporary home for two Dalmatian puppies used in the shoot, making life considerably more complicated than usual for the signalman in residence. The night would have been rather less long had the puppies acted on cue and gone back to look through the railings at the top of the box steps – I mean, how hard can it be? 'A puppy is for life,' sighed the cameraman. 'Not just for one shot.'

Harry Potter was the biggest franchise of the time, and the Bluebell was given a small bite of that enormous cherry to supply some of the sound track for the Hogwarts Express. Students of the Hogwarts Academy of Witchcraft and Wizardry arrived there each term by train, the steam-hauled Hogwarts Express departing from Platform 9¾ at King's Cross station. This platform is, of course, only accessible to witches and wizards, and invisible to even the most persistent enthusiast. Filming took place on the North Yorkshire Moors Railway, with Goathland station becoming Hogwarts with a false background. Bluebell engine *Camelot* undertook some spirited runs along Freshfield Bank, with recordings taken from the footplate and the lineside. Bluebell director Neil Glaskin also provided a selection of station noises, slamming doors and wheeling porter's trolleys about for all he was worth.

Oscar Wilde's *The Importance of Being Earnest* is as popular in the twenty-first century as it was in the nineteenth, with the part of Lady Bracknell and her delivery of the famous 'A handbag?' line still much coveted by actresses of a certain age. In 2001 it was made into a feature film by Important Films, and Horsted Keynes played the part of Victoria station. The story centres around a foundling baby discovered in a handbag on that particular station ... 'on the Brighton side', of course.

Dame Judi Dench played the principal character, Lady Bracknell, with Colin Firth as Jack and a special guest appearance by former BR chairman Sir Peter Parker as a humble railway porter. The 01 No. 65, with 'Metropolitan Railway' emblazoned on its tender sides, hauled a vintage train that would have been an unusual sight at Victoria, even in those days.

Costume and make-up are adjusted for Dame Judi Dench in *The Importance of Being Ernest.*

Also in 2001, Shepperton Studios came to the railway to make a comedy entitled *Two Men Go To War*. It tells the story of two army dentists from Aldershot who decide that there is more to being a war hero than pulling teeth and go off to France on their own initiative to take part in the action. Sheffield Park represented Aldershot, and Horsted Keynes Plymouth, where they steal a boat to take them across to France, having arrived there on a train hauled by *Blackmoor Vale*.

In 2005, the First World War came to Horsted Keynes, to take on the dual role of Gare du Nord in Paris and Nebraska for a film entitled *Flyboys*. Twenty American boys volunteer to fight for France during the early years of the war (long before the Yanks got round to joining in themselves) and end up becoming America's first fighter pilots. Horsted Keynes Platforms 3 and 4 became Gare du Nord, where injured soldiers were awaiting transport home from the front. One of the actors had once passed out by a railway line and was run over by a train, losing a leg – he had since made a decent living as a wounded soldier in war films. Platform 5 became Nebraska, where horses, cars, and covered waggons gave a flavour of the Wild West, so that it was possible, on the day, to walk from Paris to Nebraska in the blink of an eye.

In 1860s Japan, during the reign of Emperor Meiji, the emperor urged his subjects to 'seek knowledge and wisdom all over the world, that you might help to place the empire on a firm foundation'. To this end, a hundred samurai came to England and a select group of five, the Chōshū Five, was sent out specifically to search out information about the railway

Horsted Keynes becomes a busy Paris Gare du Nord station as wounded soldiers await the Ambulance Train.

system, so that this knowledge could be used to set up a similar system in Japan. We do it the other way around these days, of course, which is probably as good a testament as any to the success of the Chōshū Five. In 2006, a film was made about them and Horsted Keynes was used as the setting for their arrival in England, surrounded by Bluebell volunteers (the male ones) in top hats, tail coats, and impressive facial hair.

*Miss Potter* was a film based on the life of writer Beatrix Potter, about whose private life little is known. American actress Renée Zellweger starred as a rather twee Beatrix Potter with Ewan McGregor as her publisher, Norman Warne. Most of the film was shot in London but the production team came to Horsted Keynes to film the station scenes, which depict Beatrix leaving Norman at Euston to travel back to distant Windermere with her parents.

Sherlock Holmes hadn't been to the Bluebell since his portrayal by Jeremy Brett in the late 1980s, and in 2009 he didn't come again, but the railway was used to fill in blue-screen backgrounds for *Sherlock Holmes 2*, the follow up to *Sherlock Holmes*, an updated version of the Conan Doyle classic, with Jude Law in the title role. All that was required was a series of shots of the line from various angles; no train was needed, just our diesel shunter with a brake van and wagons for the equipment, and a helicopter filming from above.

The BBC made a children's film for television, *Station Jim*, set in the days of the older Queen Victoria, with an intelligent and ebullient Jack Russell terrier as its central character. He begins life as Chico, a performing dog in what is described in the script as 'a scruffy, small time fair'.

Our vintage fairground proprietor friends, Harris' Fair of Ashington, West Sussex, appeared in this role, the fair peopled by a few Bluebell volunteers appearing as scruffy, small-time extras. Harris' Fair has been travelling the south of England since the Victorian era and attended many Bluebell rallies, steam fairs and Victorian events over the years – they may not have agreed to the part had they read the script first!

Chico runs away from the fair and his cruel owners, who happen to be small-time villains, revolutionaries plotting against the Crown. He fetches up at Whatmidwell station, where he is adopted by Bob the porter and Henry, a young resident of the local orphanage, and renamed Jim.

The film unit spent a month at Kingscote station in October 2000, filming the adventures of Jim, Bob, and Henry and their attempts to save the orphanage from the clutches of Mr Reardon, who wants to turn it into a hotel. Stationmaster Pope (George Cole) isn't initially keen on Jim, but changes his mind once the dog catches the moles that have been plaguing him in his garden.

'Give him a book of Rules – he's staff!'

When Henry runs away and tries to 'go home' through the tunnel it is Jim who alerts Bob. It is too late for the signalman to stop the express, but Bob manages to get into the tunnel and find Henry as the express, hauled by the C Class No. 592, thunders through in an atmospheric shot shrouded in darkness and steam.

Jim's finest hour occurs during the visit of Queen Victoria (Prunella Scales) to Whatmidwell station, where she is to disembark to be driven to Montsford Hall.

On the big day of the queen's visit, Jim eventually manages to save the day, the queen, and the orphanage. Preparations for filming this scene were elaborate and not nearly as 'low key' as local residents and railway staff had been led to believe. The road outside

Kingscote station was gritted and closed to the public, so that the royal entourage could travel in a stately fashion. The Victorian royal train was hauled by the C Class No. 592, which was dressed with garlands of fresh hydrangeas and laurel leaves and carried the genuine royal coat of arms, courtesy of our museum.

Before the royal train arrives, two revolutionaries from the fair appear – the pair who once worked Jim as a performing dog. They hold the signalman at knife point in the signal box and train a gun out of the window, aimed at the forecourt where Queen Victoria will meet the station staff. The royal train arrives, and the queen alights, with her own dog on a lead. She is watching Jim perform his old fairground tricks when the pair in the box recognise him as their old Chico. The man with the gun takes a shot at the queen; Jim trips her up so that she falls to the ground, Bob losing his balance with her and shielding her from the shot, which misses everyone. Jim then runs to the box and tackles the gunman. The signalman deals with his unsavoury wife and the police arrive to take them both away. Queen Victoria becomes a patron of the orphanage, Bob is promoted to Head Porter, and Henry and Jim depart for pastures new in the brake van of a passing goods train, waving to their friends as they disappear into the tunnel. All's well that ends well.

*Above left*: Jack Russell 'Station Jim' with porter Bob Gregson (Charlie Creed-Miles).

*Above right*: Timothy West as Sir Christopher Ellis.

Queen Victoria (Prunella Scales) with (left) Stationmaster Pope (George Cole) and the Queen's Equerry (Graham Seed).

# Blowing up Trains in the Middle of the Night

During the early 2000s, two films about the French Resistance movement were made at the railway, both of which involved blowing up trains, one along a lonely stretch of line and one in the yard at Sheffield Park.

It was inevitable that Sebastian Faulks' acclaimed novel *Charlotte Gray* would be made into a film sooner or later, and in the spring of 2001 the Bluebell became the setting for one of the most exciting scenes in the film. The company set up camp for two nights near Caseford Bridge, while Sheffield Park became King's Cross. For the station shots, No. 73082 *Camelot* arrives with a train from the direction of the south into a platform crowded with military personnel, the bookshop in the background cleverly disguised as a tearoom.

The 9F No. 92240 hauled a German munitions train carrying tanks, lorries and ammunition through occupied France. It is targeted by the Resistance, Charlotte Gray prominent among them, who place explosives on the line, blowing up the two ammunition vans; the train is derailed by the explosion and falls down the embankment on its side. In the gunfire that follows, Charlotte and most of the gang get away, although one is severely injured.

The special-effects department of the film company moved into the old engine shed at Sheffield Park to build two Continental vans, one on a PMV underframe and one on an open wagon frame. The vans were constructed of balsa wood and strawboard, with wooden metal struts and hundreds of wooden boltholes glued on. The PMV had a tilting frame, hydraulically operated, to tip up at the moment of explosion. The German train was blown up between Caseford Bridge and Three Arch Bridge at around 3 a.m. Then, both exploded vans were rebuilt the following day, and the same scene was re-enacted that night. Heavy rain had made the vans somewhat soggy before the first explosion, but on the second night the vans were drier, and, in order to make sure, more explosive was used – to good effect. The second explosion was most spectacular, and the detritus was spread along the line for some distance. A small boy at the village school in Horsted Keynes, who lived near the line, informed me that he was woken up by the bang, and he had seen bits of brake van in the trees the following morning. He'd thoroughly enjoyed it. Not so other residents of the village, some of whom made their opinions known about the new Bluebell habit of 'blowing up trains in the middle of the night without telling anyone about it'– the plans to do so had, for the sake of not attracting too much attention, been kept under wraps.

The derailment of the train and the rolling down the bank wasn't filmed at Bluebell on that occasion, but in a car park in Chertsey.

In 2003 a Canadian film company spent two nights at Sheffield Park filming *Head in the Clouds*. The loco yard became a French marshalling yard, where the German army was assembling munitions trains among the engines, rolling stock and old boilers. The snowplough was painted in camouflage and fitted with a machine-gun nest, and Standard Class 4 tank No. 80064 was heavily disguised to pull a munitions train.

A small group of Resistance fighters plants a bomb under the train, hiding in the pit underneath an engine before making their getaway through the collection of boilers, pursued (and some of them captured) by soldiers with machine guns. The train, meanwhile, departs in the direction of the pump-house siding at Sheffield Park and blows up spectacularly in the background.

The German military train with its balsa-wood vans trundles by at 3 a.m. prior to being blown up and alarming the neighbours!

The explosion was the biggest set off at the Bluebell, and was heard as far away as Uckfield! There were four large thunderclap explosions in succession, followed by a large ball of fire and further explosions of dummy ammunition. The effects were even more far-reaching than the *Charlotte Gray* big bang. The roof of the adjoining old dairy melted in the intense heat, and two sheep jumped into the River Ouse. The staff at the dairy next door were watching from the safety of the road and the production manager's glasses were blown off, never to be found again.

The railway's snowplough is heavily disguised for its role in *Head in the Clouds*.

# Hammer Horror at Horsted Keynes

## *The Woman in Black* and *Angel of Death*

In October 2010 a location film unit from Hammer Horror spent several nights at the railway filming scenes for a cinema version of the ghost story by Susan Hill, which had been a successful West End play for a number of years. It starred Daniel Radcliffe (his first cinema role after leaving Hogwarts as Harry Potter) as Arthur Kipps, Liz White as Jennet Humfrye (the Woman in Black) and Ciarán Hinds as Mr Daily, all of whom were at the railway.

Set in the North East in the late Victorian era, Arthur Kipps is a young and ambitious solicitor, sent to an isolated house at the end of a causeway to wind up the estate of a recently deceased and rather eccentric client, Mrs Drablow. He attends her funeral out of courtesy, along with her local lawyer and one other mourner, a young woman wearing old-fashioned mourning dress.

However, the lawyer is most upset when Arthur asks who the woman is – he hadn't seen her, and refused to discuss her presence. Once at Mrs Drablow's house at the end of the causeway (Eel Marsh House), sorting out her effects and papers, Arthur sees the woman again in the small family graveyard attached to the house. Upon returning to the village of Crythin Gifford for supplies to stay in the house for a few days, he finds that none of his acquaintances there will discuss the woman in black, changing the subject whenever he mentions her, and they all try most strongly to dissuade him from returning to the house. Return he does, of course – young men never have any sense – to a series of ever more sinister and disturbing events, once he is alone in the house with Jennet Humfrye and her malevolence. He is eventually dragged out, more dead than alive himself, by Mr Daily, who finally tells him the terrible purpose of the Woman in Black.

It took the unit several days to dress Horsted Keynes station as Crythin Gifford station, which caused some confusion at the time, as Warner Brothers were also filming for *Sherlock Holmes 2* during that time. All the filming took place at night, usually working from about 5 p.m. to 4 a.m. Some of the scenes from the beginning of the story were shot at Sheffield Park, posing as Homerby station, where Arthur begins his journey to the wilds of Crythin Gifford. He is the only passenger on the ancient and rather slow train, taking him into the unknown on a dark, wet night, until he is joined in his carriage by Mr Daily, who befriends him. It was actually raining heavily on the night in question, but a rain rig was still erected to add to the deluge, and elaborate sets were built to cover up the south end wall of the station building, even though the camera was looking the other way.

The scenes filmed at Horsted Keynes (Crythin Gifford) took place at the end of the story, once Arthur believed himself to be free from the malignant influence of Jennet Humfrye. Turns out he thought wrong.

The film ends with dramatic scenes of Arthur's young son Joseph (Arthur is a widower whose wife died in childbirth), played by Radcliffe's godson Misha Handley, being run over by a train and snatched from under its wheels by his father at the last minute – or possibly not. Arthur, Joseph, and Joseph's nanny arrive at Crythin Gifford station to take the train home, and Joseph wanders off while his father and nanny are engaged in buying tickets. Under the influence of the Woman in Black, who appears on the opposite platform, he climbs down onto the railway line and walks towards the oncoming train. Changes in the lighting at this point transform the atmosphere on the station from the everyday, when the family is arriving and buying tickets, to the sinister and other worldly as 'she' appears on the scene.

This scene was filmed in several different ways; a camera track was laid inside the 'four foot' (the space between the rails) for several yards, and while Misha stood unflinchingly at the end of it, the rolling camera hurtled towards him, giving an engine's eye view of the disaster. Then the engine was filmed coming towards a large mirror, with a dazzling white lamp on the front. Not very authentic, of course, but being dazzled by the oncoming train was a vital part of the whole effect ... and it's not easy to be dazzled by an oil lamp.

The final scene was filmed down on the track between the platforms and featured Arthur Kipps, Joseph, Arthur's wife Stella, and a group of ghost children, who had fallen under Jennet Humfrye's spell.

The children were filming until long after midnight on a cold night in flimsy garments, silently following Arthur, as he leads them away from 'her' powerful influence towards the afterlife, which lies, as we always suspected, somewhere north of Horsted Keynes. The children themselves didn't make the final cut, which focused only on Arthur and Joseph, reunited in death with Joseph's mother, the Woman in Black screaming at them from the platform.

News soon reached the sleepy village of Horsted Keynes that Harry Potter was in town, which caused quite a stir. The children of Elm Class at St Giles' School wrote a letter to Daniel Radcliffe and included a self-portrait by each child. In a brief interval between takes one night, Radcliffe was kind enough to write back to them, including a self-portrait of

Daniel Radcliffe's first cinema role after finding fame as Harry Potter – Arthur Kipps in *The Woman in Black*.

The ghost children walk on the line towards the afterlife.

himself as Harry Potter. Both the original letter and its reply occupied pride of place in the school entrance for parents' evening that week.

In 2014 a sequel was made to *The Woman in Black*, entitled *Angel of Death*. Susan Hill never wrote a sequel, but somebody in the film industry obviously considered Eel Marsh House too good to be consigned to horror history after just one film.

This story is set many years after the original Victorian horror, during the Second World War. Some children are evacuated to Eel Marsh House, which is, of course, still haunted by the Woman in Black. Horsted Keynes station featured early on in their adventure, as they are transferred from the train to the bus that will take them to their wartime billet. The booking hall was elaborately dressed for the scene to appear derelict and suffering the neglect of many years. Dust and ashes from an old fire in the grate were scattered over the floor, and dead flies (a large box of them had been provided) were sprinkled over the mantelpiece and the windowsills. A tatty, yellowing lace curtain was suspended on a string across one window, and another was broken, with the glass left on the floor, and the children's bus seen through the jagged hole. This done, the principal child actor went sick (after a drowning scene had given him the flu) and the booking hall had to remain 'in character' until the following week. Horsted station staff spent a busy weekend explaining to passengers that, no, the booking hall didn't usually look like this, and yes, they did know about the broken window ...

# The Invisible Woman

## Charles Dickens and the Staplehurst Disaster of 1865

On 9 June 1865, the boat train from Folkestone was travelling through Kent, due to reach Headcorn at 3.15 p.m. On board, the prestigious author Charles Dickens was looking over his manuscript of *Our Mutual Friend,* putting a few finishing touches to the breakfast party with the Laramies and the Boffins. It was a bright, sunny day, and neither Dickens, his fellow passengers, or the engine crew could have had any inkling of what lay ahead.

Near Staplehurst, a tracklaying gang was relaying rail in between trains on a viaduct over a small river.

A concatenation of mistakes by the foreman was building towards a disaster with fatal consequences. The boat train was timed to fit in with the tides and did not run at the same time every day; and although the foreman had a timetable, he had misread it and then it had been run over by a previous train. He thought the boat train was due to reach Headcorn at 5.20 p.m. and had planned to have the rails in place by 4.15 p.m. As the previous few days' work had proceeded smoothly, the foreman was regarded by L. T. C. Rolt, author of railway accident compendium *Red for Danger*, as 'looking upon the business of protection as a mere formality'. A look-out man was posted a mere 550 yards from the viaduct and, although he had detonators, he had been told not to use them unless it was foggy.

When the express approached at 50 mph, two lengths of rail were still out. By the time the driver saw the look-out's red flag, it was too late to do anything about it. Incredibly, the engine, tender and leading brake van managed to cross the rail-less gap on the underlying timber baulks, but five coaches fell over the viaduct down the bank, one being upended and one upside down in the river. Ten people died and about fifty were injured.

In June 2012, the same month as the accident, it was recreated on the Bluebell's Ardingly spur at Horsted Keynes as part of a film about the double life of Charles Dickens, with his wife and large family and with his mistress Nelly Ternan. The film was directed by Ralph Fiennes, who also played Dickens, and dwelt mainly on the central relationship between Dickens and young Nelly, the story fleshed out with many, many lingering shots of the heroine's elegant, swanlike neck.

For the train crash, visiting engine Furness Railway No. 20, built in 1864, was hired in to haul the Victorian train. Sheffield Park played the part of Folkestone, and the passing shots of the train were taken as it ran from Three Arch Bridge towards Sheffield Park. The train was too heavy for the engine to start again on the gradient, so, having come to a stand, it was assisted back up to Horsted Keynes for another go.

The crash site took two weeks to construct. Three replica carriages were built down the steep bank of the Ardingly spur: one upside down at the bottom, one upended at the top, and one on its side and impaled on a tree halfway down. During the building, care was taken to disturb the site as little as possible, as it had to appear that the train had careered down a steep, wooded bank overgrown with trees. The replica carriages weren't models knocked up out of chipboard – the construction and detail were stunning. The upturned coach was complete with every detail of the underframe, including the battery boxes, which would not have been on the original train, but were on the real one. Both of the other coaches were lavishly upholstered, all the lining out was in place, as were door handles, handrails, and window blinds.

The filming at the crash site centred on Dickens emerging from the train, shaken but unscathed, to go to the aid of fellow passengers. As he staggers down the bank to the scene of devastation, the props and make-up departments show their work. Scattered around the crashed coaches are cases and holdalls, umbrellas, coats, and even a violin and its case. The wounded and dying lay in and out of the wreckage; one woman had had her throat cut as she went through the window, and a dead ticket inspector was sprawled under the upturned coach. Alan Middleton and Tim Owen, the driver and fireman who came with the Furness engine down from Cumbria, were dressed and made up with minor cuts and whiskers to play their part. Tim ran down the bank to assist the passengers and Alan was directed to stand at the top and assume the expression of a driver viewing a catastrophe that had been his fault. He pointed out, quite correctly, that the accident hadn't been his fault, but that of the foreman platelayer, and assumed instead the expression of a driver viewing a catastrophe that was someone else's fault.

Watching the rushes on the screen in the catering tent, the desolation of the scene came across very well. The desperation of the passengers was easy to understand – how would you go about getting help for several dying and seriously injured people at the bottom of a steep railway bank in the middle of nowhere in 1865?

The actual crash was filmed in the studio in a mock-up carriage interior, cutting seamlessly to the scenes of devastation on the railway bank. It looked so like a real train that everyone at the railway concurred that the site of the crash was well chosen – had the 'crash' been in view of the public there would have been a local outcry, and the Bluebell's passenger numbers may well have suffered a steep decline.

Dickens later wrote:

On Friday the ninth of June in the present year, Mr and Mrs Boffin (in their manuscript dress of receiving Mr and Mrs Laramie at breakfast) were on the South

Ralph Fiennes, director and star (Charles Dickens) of *The Invisible Woman*.

The 1865 Staplehurst crash recreated at the Bluebell.

Eastern Railway with me, in a terribly destructive accident. When I had done what I could to help others, I climbed back into my carriage – nearly turned over a viaduct, and caught aslant upon the turn – to extricate the worthy couple. They were much soiled, but otherwise unhurt. I remember with devout thankfulness that I can never be much nearer parting company with my readers forever than I was then.

## Muppetry

The Victorian elegance of Horsted Keynes station lends itself well as a backdrop to such well-known, quality productions as *Downton Abbey, Poirot, Sherlock Holmes,* and *Jeeves and Wooster* – the Muppets in *Muppets Most Wanted,* maybe not so much. Indeed, Horsted Keynes station must be one of the unlikeliest of locations for this Walt Disney extravaganza, but the production team took over the station for a week's filming in March 2013, plus a week prior for set dressing and one after for undressing.

The main task for the scaffolders and riggers who preceded the production crew was to erect a 'blue screen' along the whole length of the carriage shed, while another gang prepared the train and the engine, *Baxter,* for their starring role. The train had been selected some time previously, when the director had ventured bravely into the C&W

graveyard in the sidings and picked out the most dilapidated and decrepit vehicles that he could see (the less paint adhering to them and the more bits missing the better), and stipulated that as long as the wheels went round, that was all that was required. Not the usual criteria by which film directors choose their trains.

Once hacked out of the brambles and extricated from the back of beyond, the train was painted with scenes depicting a travelling circus of the old-fashioned type, replete with elephants, tigers, clowns, and acrobats; the paint then dirtied down to look faded and weathered.

*Baxter* was also in for a treat. Renamed *Randy Stevenot*, the engine was adorned with a smokestack, large brass whistle, front headlamp, cow catcher, and a set of stars and stripes.

In the film, the Muppets are off on a world tour, organised by their new manager Dominic (Ricky Gervais) – a wrong 'un in league with criminal mastermind Constantine, Kermit's double. The tour has been arranged to cover their activities in banks and strongholds near to the theatres on the tour, but the Muppets, of course, are ignorant of all this. Kermit has promised them a train for the tour, and they arrive all eager and expectant at the station in Los Angeles, breathless with excitement as a brand-new silver Amtrak train pulls out, and behind it … yup, that's their train. No particular historical period is indicated – the steam train, apparently, merely denotes (perhaps unfairly) age and decrepitude.

So off they set on their world tour, bits falling off the train regularly en route. Horsted is Berlin and Dublin, depending on which posters were pasted up at the time – and that blue screen along the carriage shed was to have the Los Angeles skyline projected onto it.

Once the scene was set, the big stars arrived. Kermit the Frog, Miss Piggy, Fozzie Bear, Waldorf and Statler, Scooter, Sweetums, Animal … they were all there. Ricky Gervais was among the great and the good, the only actor not to be wrapped in a bin bag and bundled into the waiting room when not required on set. They were all filmed boarding the train (Miss Piggy with far too much luggage) and on board the train, with Beauregard as the driver.

Lineside shots were taken south of Horsted Keynes to depict the Irish countryside on the approach to Dublin. This was no simple task, as there were four men in the cab of *Baxter* (driver, fireman, director, and muppeteer), none of whom could be visible to the camera. They all had to spend the journey – thankfully short – on the cab floor, and *Baxter* is not a roomy engine.

Criminal mastermind Constantine has escaped from Gulag, and had Kermit imprisoned in his place, unnoticed by any of the Muppets – at first. Then Walter becomes suspicious and follows Dominic one evening in Dublin to find out that, in order to ensure that the noise from the theatre drowns out the drilling and dynamiting in the bank next door, he has been bribing journalists in the cities that they have visited to write rave reviews of the Muppet Show and paying people to attend the performances.

Walter, Animal, and Fozzie are then onto Dominic and Constantine, and have to escape from the Muppet train to save their lives – and Kermit.

In the only stunt at the Bluebell where the risk assessment made no mention of injury to the actors, the three of them leap from their stationary train in Platform 2 to a passing freight train hauled by a diesel shunter as it hurtled through Platform 3, on their way out of Dublin to Russia and Gulag prison.

*Muppets Most Wanted* may not be one of the most classic movies to come out of the Bluebell film studio, but it was certainly one of the most enjoyable, and worth watching for the train scenes.

*Baxter* becomes *Randy Stevenot* with some US-style additions for *Muppets Most Wanted*. A blue screen was erected in order that the train would be projected against a Los Angeles skyline.

'Birdcage' Brake coach No. 1061 in its circus livery. Some stunning artwork was applied to the railway's most decrepit coaches.

# 14

# The 2010s

## Adverts are Back

Adverts had fallen out of favour at the Bluebell during the 1990s and into the new millennium, but into the 2010s they enjoyed a resurgence. The chocolate biscuits, Ford Escorts and Walkmans of old were firmly in the past, and mobile-phone networks and credit cards took their place, with adverts for online services that can be used during travel becoming popular.

In 2013 Channel 4 made an advert for On Demand, which featured a couple waiting on a seat at an isolated railway station, awaiting their delayed train and becoming more and more bored as they pass the time with a word puzzle.

The location crew mentioned in passing that they wanted a location for a building site, somewhere in the vicinity of the railway, and were soon installed in the Permanent Way yard at Horsted, having provided their own bricks, cement mixer, scaffolding, barrows, and actors with bum cleavages.

Hyundai credit cards in 2015 and Utility Cashback in 2020 both used famous faces to promote the product. Actor Tom Hardy was Hyundai's 'man on the train' and was flown in by chopper from Pinewood at great expense and no little inconvenience. The helicopter was supposed to land at the top end of the field at Horsted Keynes, but overhead telephone wires prompted the pilot to make a last-minute decision to land in an adjacent field. A minibus had been provided to transport Hardy from the chopper to the unit base, about 100 yards away. Due to the hastily revised landing arrangements, the great actor (who has appeared in a few action movies) had to walk from the helicopter across a muddy field and negotiate brambles and a barbed wire fence, all without a stunt double, to make it through to the minibus for the last few yards.

National treasure Joanna Lumley made her Utility Warehouse cashback card advert just before lockdown in February 2020 with much less fuss. With her trademark elegance, she graced the platform at Kingscote, walking through the station and out to the forecourt to drive away in her car.

A couple of adverts featured phones on trains for Vodafone and O2. Vodafone advertised the facility to watch the latest film on your phone – wherever you are. Martin

The ever-elegant Joanna Lumley at Kingscote in 2020.

Freeman is the hacked-off commuter looking forward to seeing the latest film release when he goes home, only to find everyone on the train watching it on their phones. He is moved to shout out, 'What is wrong with you people?' as he tries to find somewhere away from the film on other people's phones to sit. A Mk 2 carriage hired from the Mid-Norfolk Railway was used for the interior, and the final seconds of the advert showed the train passing though Horsted Keynes, albeit a Horsted Keynes with lots more lines and a different background to the one with which we are familiar. Mr Freeman need have had no worries about his spoiler alert, for Horsted Keynes has no phone signal – from Vodafone or anyone else!

The little blue O2 robot put in an appearance at Horsted Keynes during the summer of 2020 as lockdown was eased. His friend on this occasion was a young woman carrying a cello in a case as she rushes up the subway steps on a rainy day just in time to see her train depart. The little robot rushes back down the steps and out of the station entrance to hail a passing taxi, which splashes through a puddle, giving him a good soaking.

A day's prep was needed to transform Horsted Keynes into a present-day station with modern seating, a digital destination board, and no character whatsoever. No detail was omitted – the props dept even brought their own fake pothole for the puddle scene, even though the station drive has plenty of its own.

Not wearing a mask during lockdown: the 02 robot.

## Dove Chocolates

The Bluebell was approached to make an advert for Dove chocolates in December 2014, for the Chinese market. Some negotiation was needed regarding the location, but finally the film crew agreed to Kingscote, once it was pointed out (firmly) that the other stations were decorated for Christmas and weren't going to be undecorated for anyone.

Kingscote was then decorated for Chinese New Year with strings of lanterns, and the vintage set, hauled by *Birch Grove* between Kingscote and Vaux End, provided the setting for the action.

A young woman is travelling home to her parents for New Year, although we never got to the bottom of why she was on board an English steam train. It seemed to be loosely connected to the popularity of *Downton Abbey* in China at the time – they had initially asked for 'the Downton train'. Opposite the young woman in her fashionable coat was seated an old woman in an old-fashioned Chinese jacket, placidly knitting with a box of Dove chocolates in an open bag beside her – clearly not disposed to part with them.

When they alight from the train at Kingscote, where her parents are waiting, the young woman is wearing the old Chinese jacket and carrying the box of chocolates, and the old woman attired in the stylish, modern coat. As the girl shares the chocolates with her parents, New Year fireworks (actually coloured lights) go off in the background.

A couple of boxes of Dove chocolates ended up in our front room over Christmas; we opened a box to accompany a *Minder* DVD by the fire to find that each chocolate had been stuck down to the plastic tray with double-sided tape so that the box could be tipped up on camera without them falling out. Tasted fine though.

## Go Compare

At one time, no location worth its salt had escaped without a visit from the waved hair, twirled moustachiod, white tie and tails of Gio Compario, played by Welsh tenor Wynne Evans. The Bluebell was no exception.

In June 2015 he turned up with a crew of sixty to film a Go Compare car-insurance commercial with a *Brief Encounter* flavour. With a vintage train drawn up in the platform at Horsted Keynes, three couples ballroom dance along its length as a husband speaks to his wife through the window of the just-arrived train, asking her why she travelled by rail.

'Because she can't afford the car insurance', of course. Cue Gio Compario bursting out of the next window along with his usual refrain. The couple then dance out through the station entrance to the forecourt, where a Triumph Roadster is parked. And not any old Triumph Roadster – the 1947 version used by John Nettles as Jim Bergerac in the 1980s.

As the couple get in and set off down the drive, Gio appears again, popping up on the dickey seat, tooting a motor horn and singing 'Go Compare', though not before anyone thought to remove the 2015 tax disc from the car windscreen.

Gio Compario, star of the long-running Go Compare adverts.

## Smart Forrail

In June 2015 Mercedes Benz launched its new four-seater Smart car and came up with a novel and ingenious way to publicise it. The ideal mode of transport, they decided, would combine the comfort and privacy of one's own car with the speed and directness of an empty railway line – if only it could be done.

Interfleet engineers at Derby converted one of the new cars to run on rails, taking six months to design and construct it. They made solid steel wheels, heavy enough to give enough traction on the rails. The steering was disconnected, and aluminium supports were welded between the axles to lock the wheels in position. All they needed now was a railway line ...

A short film was made with the Smart Forrail car running from Sheffield Park to East Grinstead, 'driven' by the MD of Mercedes Benz, with a Bluebell driver in attendance. As the signals clear, the car leaves Sheffield Park, the driver reading the paper and eating a packet of Haribos as it progresses in glorious solitude along the line. It passes S15 No. 847 at Kingscote and continues to the viaduct, where a drone provides some impressive shots of the little yellow car dwarfed by the Victorian structure as it enters East Grinstead station, where the driver 'detrains', so to speak, and drives away in a conventional Smart car.

The Smart car adapted to run on rails.

The young man leaves for war and says his goodbyes to his girlfriend. (Hornby)

## Hornby Centenary

Hornby celebrated its centenary in 2020 and brought out a short film to commemorate the event. It opens with a small boy in the 1920s receiving his first basic circular train set and a simple LNER tank engine. He grows up, and, as a young man, goes off to war from Sheffield Park station. His sweetheart gives him a parting gift, which he opens on the train – his old childhood engine in a box.

Having survived the war, the film changes to colour for the 1950s and 1960s to see the young man through marriage and a first home, with Hornby engines on the mantelpiece and the moon landing on TV. He goes through a rough patch after that, enduring the pain of 1970s wallpaper and the need to sell his original engine (for £85). All ends happily, however, on his 100th birthday, as, surrounded by his family, he receives another train set as a gift, almost a century after the first.

## Gucci

A money-no-object fashion shoot for the Italian fashion house's autumn/winter children's collection took over Horsted Keynes station as a backdrop for four days in March 2020. At that time, the pandemic was looming – yet to hit Britain in a big way, but Italy was already going into lockdown and the big guns of Gucci were unable to leave the country and had to do their directing via video link, a precursor to the Zoom era that was soon to envelop us all.

01 No. 65 and the vintage Met Set provided the background for the children in a variety of smart, weird, and wonderful attire, surrounded by old wooden toys and vast numbers of

plants and shrubs – the haul of a haphazard raid on the local garden centre. Backgrounds included the engine and train, the station and booking office, and a teetering pile of vintage luggage, some pristine (courtesy of Gucci props department) and some battered (courtesy of Horsted Keynes station).

After a final cheerful picture of all the children peering out of the same carriage window and waving, wooden engines and hobby horses piled on the platform, the shoot was wrapped. That was the last film job before lockdown, and the last time, for a while, that children would be able to cram together at a train window and wave to assembled crowds.

Storm clouds were gathering as the pandemic took hold, and the film crew left in rather more than the usual hurry at the end of the shoot, abandoning the garden centre in their wake. We still refer to our front garden as the Gucci Garden.

Vintage luggage piled high for Gucci's children's collection advert.

## 'Listen to the Silence'

In July 2020 a German band, Amistat, made a music video, taking advantage of lockdown and the closure of the Bluebell to use Sharpthorne Tunnel and the empty railway line as a setting. A small crew of six, out of doors and socially distanced, complied with all the rules laid down (but clearly not adhered to) by the government, and with railway rules, working under an engineer's possession. A young couple explored the tunnel, hopped along the sleepers, balanced along the rails and sat outside the platelayer's hut. The quiet and dark of the tunnel contrasted with sun-drenched pastoral peace of the deserted railway line. The title of the song, 'Listen to the Silence', was particularly poignant in the middle of July, when the line and tunnel would normally have been buzzing with passing trains.

## Television

The Bluebell Railway appeared on TV screens as itself a few times during this decade, in programmes relating to various eras from the 1930s to the present day, and Channel 5 film crews were never away from the place.

In October 2014, the popular daytime TV reality show *Escape to the Country* found its way to the railway. The show takes a couple who want to move to the countryside and finds them several houses in their chosen catchment area. To add background, the presenters explore the area and its attractions. The couple then looks at the houses, weighs up the pros and cons of all of them, has a great time at the programme's expense, and doesn't buy any of them. The presenters must know that this will happen every time, but it never seems to dampen their enthusiasm.

For this episode, presenter Sonali Shah accompanied a couple looking at properties in West Chiltington, Amberley, and Nutbourne, and the Bluebell was considered as a main local attraction, so Sonali spent the day at the railway sampling its delights. She arrived at East Grinstead, rode on the train, and joined the crew on the footplate of S15 No. 847. She ended up at Sheffield Park and somehow got involved in lighting up the P Class *Bluebell*, ready for the next day.

The film crew moved on to film the Jack and Jill windmills at Clayton on the South Downs. The couple did not, of course, buy any of the properties.

In 2015 the BBC made a documentary, *First Days of Peace*, which explored the eagerness of Britons to get their beaches back as holiday resorts after the end of the Second World War. The coastal towns of Sussex and Kent were suddenly called upon to handle the new demand after years of being England's front line of defence against invasion. Filming took place on the service train to provide some background to the story and interview people with memories of that time. Presumably, all coastal towns were expected to go through this sudden metamorphosis; the beaches of Walmington-on-Sea must have lost their barbed wire and mines at about this time, and the Novelty Rock Emporium and the Orphans Sunshine Holiday Home restored to the purposes for which they were intended.

In 2019, Channel 5 made a documentary, *Secrets of the Royal Train*. The royal train is a famous British institution, and this documentary followed its 150-year history since Queen Victoria first boarded her palace on wheels. During the First World War it delivered the king across the country to visit his subjects in time of peril – something that could not have been achieved in the pre-railway era. The train was armoured during the Second World War and then updated to the highest standards of modernity afterwards. Further refurbishments in the 1970s and 1980s were more modest.

Scenes of the royal train were interspersed with shots of various steam trains, and Q Class No. 541 at the Bluebell was filmed to add background. The engine was filmed running round and watering at Sheffield Park, and a few shots of axle boxes being lifted from the H Class in the workshop. The programme presenter had mentioned that the main requirement for a royal train driver was the ability to stop in the right place for the red carpet, so driver Roland Law demonstrated the necessary skill for this, with a carpet placed on the platform.

The presenters all became a little confused, and continually referred to the royal train as 'the most famous British loco of all time', and there were shots of it being hauled by various prestigious steam locos (sadly not the Q Class). This does suggest that iconic trains are still associated with steam in the minds of the populace. And maybe they should be.

In September 2020, Channel 5 made *The 1930s in Colour*, documenting the social and economic history of the decade, using original colour film of the times. One major event was the opening of the first Butlins Holiday Camp in 1931; in 1938 a less light-hearted and more menacing film showed the German football team visiting Britain and giving a Nazi salute on the pitch.

At Sheffield Park, three former refugees were interviewed inside the train about their experiences. One of them, Dame Stephanie Shirley, came to Britain as a child refugee and went on to become a successful businesswoman, entrepreneur, and philanthropist, starting up one of the first computer companies in 1962.

Also in 2020, another Channel 5 documentary explored the part played by railways in the life and writing of Agatha Christie, presented by travel writer Simon Calder. He explained that the 1920s and 1930s were the golden age of travel, with intense competition between the Big Four. It was also the golden age of female crime writers, notably Christie, Dorothy L. Sayers and Margery Allingham. Agatha Christie enjoyed railway travel, and this was the inspiration for several of her murder mysteries.

# TV Serials

The Bluebell was the backdrop for several popular TV serials during the decade, with settings from *The Suspicions of Mr Whicher* in the Victorian era to the 1950s, and a collection of serials about the development of British industry and society in which railways played a large part.

## The Suspicions of Mr Whicher

In 2009 Kate Summerscale's book *The Suspicions of Mr Whicher* detailed the true and grisly story of the murder of a small boy by his older sister, who stuffed the body down the privy in the garden, in 1860. Detective Jack Whicher, one of the first in his profession, investigated the case, coming up against the authorities (the Victorian version of 'this is how we've always done it') constantly. His character inspired a series of fictional stories featuring Paddy Considine as the detective, and the Bluebell appeared in two of them.

In 'Beyond the Pale', set in 1865 (April 2014), he is in search of two young boys who have gone missing and eventually runs them to the ground at Victoria station, played by Horsted

Keynes. Mr Whicher was filmed on Leamland Bridge at Horsted, watching the vintage train pass by underneath. The station was set nearer to the bridge than it actually is, and passengers leaving the train passed by him as they walked over the bridge.

In May, Mr Whicher was back in another episode, 'The Ties that Bind'. This time it was the turn of Sheffield Park to play both Wainsbury and Lydford in Wiltshire, shot from opposite ends of the platform. Mr Whicher is met on the platform by Lady Mary, with various items of luggage. She is off to Bristol; Mr Whicher boards the train to Lydford, alighting (some time later) at the other end of the platform. On the train, Mr Whicher takes a letter out of his top pocket, opens and reads it, and then tears up the letter and envelope and throws them out of the window – cue lineside shots of vintage set and fluttering paper.

## Grantchester

The beautiful setting of 1950s Cambridge was the background to *Grantchester*, a mystery series with a dishy young vicar, Revd Sidney, solving murders left, right, and centre. When not helping the police with their enquiries, he was busy getting embroiled in an affair with a scheming married woman. How he found time for celebrating Communion, writing sermons, baptising, marrying, burying, attending PCC meetings, and the general work of the parish is one of the unsolved mysteries of the series.

Horsted Keynes station was the scene of an altercation between two women, Annabel and Pamela, as Annabel attempts to murder Pamela by pushing her in front of a passing train. The fight was filmed with both women perilously close to the edge of the platform (a mattress on the tracks just in case) and then shot again a few paces back with the train passing. Pamela is saved and Annabel restrained – no real harm done. In other, calmer scenes, Horsted reprised its role, played several times in the past, as Cambridge station, where two other women, Amanda and Hildegard, are waved off by Revd Sidney. He then follows the train on his bicycle, still waving.

## The Go Between and The Outcast

Things often go in cycles, and in September and October 2014 two TV serials were made, set fifty years apart, with themes of forbidden love and deceit behind a veneer of respectability. *The Go Between* is set in 1900 and tells the story of an affair between Marion and a local tenant farmer of inferior standing, Ted. Marion's younger brother has a school friend, Leo, who comes to stay in the holidays and ends up embroiled in the affair as a carrier of *billets-doux* between the pair. Filming took place on the train hauled by U Class No. 1618 (yet to be built in 1900) as Leo travelled to his holiday destination.

*The Outcast* is set just post-war and also from the viewpoint of a small boy, Lewis. His father remarries after Lewis' mother dies, and they move to a new house, where the neighbours are socially superior. Lewis befriends the children and it soon becomes clear that, behind the net curtains of 1950s respectability, all kinds of abuses lurk. Kingscote was Waterford and Horsted Keynes became Norwich. The U Class, this time in the right period, hauled a train in which the adult Lewis meets his younger self.

## Arthur & George

In November 2014 a three-parter was filmed for ITV with Martin Clunes as Sir Arthur Conan Doyle and Charles Edwards as his 'gentleman', Woody. The writer was not averse

Martin Clunes poses with the footplate crew in *Arthur & George*.

to doing a little sleuthing of his own before sleuthing had really been invented. He investigated a notorious miscarriage of justice involving a solicitor accused of mutilating animals in a case that became known, with typical Victorian understatement, as the Great Wyrley Rippings. Sheffield Park was Great Wyrley, home village of the accused, and Horsted Keynes was Crannock. Conan Doyle and Woody travelled to Great Wyrley from Crannock in the vintage train to visit the scene of the crime, hauled by P Class No. 178. Aboard the train, Conan Doyle discourses to Woody about the village of Great Wyrley as they approach it. In the pedantic manner that he handed on to Sherlock Holmes, he lists the public houses, shops and their proprietors, and the geographical features of the area. Woody, like Watson, remains politely subservient while clearly bored.

## Cuffs

In June 2015 the Bluebell played itself in a modern drama set with Sussex Police – *Cuffs*. In the story as originally planned, an elderly woman with dementia wanders into the path of a train to be rescued by a policeman, probably in the nick of time. However, the plan to lay a third rail to simulate a modern line proved too much for the budget, and the film crew had to think again. Someone came up with the inspired idea of using the Bluebell as itself, a flash of brilliance. After all, a heritage railway, in practical terms, would be far easier for an elderly lady to wander onto than a stretch of Network Rail.

The new idea also showed the esteem in which heritage railways are now held in the national psyche, as much a part of the scenery as our castles and great houses, existing in their own right and not just as a backdrop for a period drama. The elderly woman

An elderly dementia patient is rescued from the line in the police series *Cuffs*.

wandered onto the line between Kingscote and Imberhorne, where she was rescued from an unfortunate end under the wheels of the S15 No. 847.

## Churchill's Secret

In July 2015 the railway returned to the summer of 1953, in an ITV drama, *Churchill's Secret*, starring Michael Gambon as Churchill and Lindsay Duncan as his wife Clem. It focuses on the moment of that summer when Churchill, prime minister for the second time around and in his late seventies, suffers a stroke in the car on the way to Chartwell. His illness was kept a strict secret from the press and the world (something that was still achievable then) and his young nurse Millie Appleyard (Romola Garai) was sworn to secrecy. The film focuses on his struggle to recover, Clem's hope that the stroke will force him to retire, and the scheming of his political 'allies' plotting his succession. At the height of the drama, his adult children gather at Chartwell, uncertain that he will pull through, and family tensions rise to the surface.

Kingscote became Oxted, the nearest station to Chartwell, where Churchill's daughters alight from their trains and meet to travel to their father, and nurse Millie signs the Official Secrets Act.

Diana Churchill (Tara Fitzgerald) alights from the train at Oxted station for *Churchill's Secret*.

## Railways: The Making of a Nation

BBC 4 followed in the footsteps of Ruth Goodman, Peter Ginn, and Alex Langlands, moving on from the focus on the Victorian era to the development of suburbia and commuter towns. In *The Rise of the Commuter,* presenter Liz McIvor explored the development of the railways that led to urban sprawl. Surbiton was cited as an example, and John Betjeman's 1973 film *Metro-Land* was used as a background, featuring the poet in Horsted Keynes buffet, then boarding the train to 'Metro-land'. The C Class and the vintage set featured in the filming, along with the much more modern *Camelot*, and the episode ended at the Crossrail development site.

## The Railways That Built Britain with Chris Tarrant

Presenter Chris Tarrant jumped on the bandwagon in October 2016 in a programme exploring the transition from a largely rural economy to an urban one with the coming of the railways.

He focused on the labour-intensive nature of any work involving steam locos, and the length of time taken to progress from cleaner to driver. He spent some time in the workshop looking at loco construction and then moved out into the yard to experience the long-winded nature of engine prep. There he found out why it generally takes about three hours from the cleaning out of the smokebox and grate of a large engine in the morning to its eventual arrival on the front of the train.

Mick Blackburn supervises Chris Tarrant cleaning out an engine smokebox. (Mike Hopps)

# The Larkins

Shall I compare thee to a summer's day?
Rough winds do shake the darling buds of May
And summer's lease hath all too short a date.

H. E. Bates' book *The Darling Buds of May*, set in Kent in the 1950s, used a line from the Shakespeare sonnet as its title. It was inspired by a single moment, witnessed by the author, on a summer day in a Kentish village. A dilapidated truck pulled up outside the village shop and disgorged its cargo of a large family, in the charge of a jovial father, who bought ice creams all round before they all piled back into the truck and drove away. The book was made into a TV series in the 1990s, with David Jason as Pop, Pam Ferris as Ma, and Catherine Zeta-Jones as Mariette. One man, later interviewed on Radio 4, watching the opening scenes and reading about H. E. Bates' moment of inspiration, realised that the sense of familiarity that he had was because it was *his* family, as he was one of the children in the truck. He even remembered the occasion, although not the author watching in the background.

Filmed in April 2021, a new TV series about the Larkin family, *The Larkins*, featuring H. E. Bates' characters with new storylines in 1950s Kent, was made for a Sunday night ITV slot. Horsted Keynes became Littlechurch station, where several scenes were filmed, running over the six episodes of the series, telling the story of the proposed closure of the station and Pop's fight to save it. Pop's first big idea was to gather a crowd at the station for an outing on the train and pay for all their tickets to create demand; his next idea was to encourage travel (and make a bit on the side) by selling Larkin strawberries, unauthorised, on the train. As the train, hauled by Q Class No. 541, is stationary in the platform, Mariette loads strawberries on board while Pop delays the departure by distracting the driver, pointing out 'something under the wheel', which the driver then has to investigate.

One of Pop's outings by train was to a 'place of educational interest' with the local school children. They travelled from Horsted to Kingscote, and the site of Chailey Windmill, which had been transported there by the power of CGI.

Meanwhile, back at the station, dark deeds are afoot. Mr Fox the stationmaster has been cooking the books in the booking office, siphoning off a sizeable share of the profits, another nail in the coffin of the station itself. Pop Larkin has found out, and the fat is well and truly in the fire. Mr Fox himself was unconcerned about the proposed closure, as he had lined his pockets in anticipation of the event, and in the scene filmed in the booking office when he is confronted by Pop, he declares, 'It's a sign of the times – branch lines are for the chop.' Prescient words indeed.

Pop's friend Katy Farley is a railway enthusiast and train spotter, and she is on the platform among the crowds that Pop had drummed up to save the station. As the train arrives, she announces that it is hauled by a 'Class 5 BR 1B' (actually the Q Class).

Finally, of course, Pop saves the station and there is a party in the booking office to celebrate. With Mr Fox safely behind bars, Katy is given the job of stationmaster, and appears proudly wearing her new uniform. Sir George and Lady Bluff-Gore mingle with the party, Sir George announcing confidently, 'Steam – that's the future!'

Bradley Walsh (Pop Larkin) and his family at Horsted Keynes.

Indeed it is, for the time being. The station and the branch line are secured, and Katy can look forward to a future in charge of Littlechurch station, happily misidentifying incoming locomotives.

The Larkins starred Bradley Walsh (Pop Larkin), Joanna Scanlan (Ma Larkin), Sabrina Bartlett (Mariette), and Tok Stephen (Charley). The series was shown on ITV during October 2021.

## Films

The railway appeared in a number of cinema films over the decade, playing its part in many settings, period and modern, thrillers, dramas, and literary adaptations.

In November 2014 the small village of West Hoathly was set astir by the arrival of a film crew in their tunnel – and Colin Firth. The spy thriller *Secret Service*, starring

Sir Michael Caine and Colin Firth, used the tunnel for several days to film a modern, thrilling version of the old favourite silent comedy 'tied to the track' routine.

Eggsy (Colin Firth), working for Michael Caine, is being tested for the qualities of courage and strength, both physical and mental, that he will need for his role in the Secret Service. He is injected with something to knock him out, and comes round tied to the railway line in a tunnel. He is interrogated by 'the enemy' but fails to crack, even as the train approaches. Just as it thunders over him, the track drops down under him, and he finds himself three feet below the underside of the train, looking up through walls of concrete. The train passes, the track rises up, and Eggsy has passed the test. The actual dropping of the track and the passing train were filmed in the studio, using a length of track from the Bluebell.

Colin Firth proved a popular visitor to West Hoathly, and was gracious enough to sign autographs for the villagers who had been congregating by the crossing all day, and for the children getting off the school bus.

The year 2017 was a busy one for the Bluebell on the big screen, as it took the cinema goer from Cambridge to Normandy, and as far afield as Amritsar Junction.

## Overlord

During the Second World War, two American paratroopers are engaged on a mission to destroy a German radio tower in a small town outside Normandy. They were fully prepared for a battle against Nazi troops, but not to find themselves pitted against the supernatural forces that are the result of strange and unwholesome Nazi experiments. They are called upon to do this in Lywood Tunnel, along the old trackbed to Ardingly. From the Bluebell's

German military vehicles outside Lywood Tunnel during filming for *Overlord*.

point of view, this was an ideal film job, as it enabled several weeks of prep and filming to take place without any disruption to train services or railway routines. There were some desperate battles in the tunnel and the surrounding woodland, culminating in a massive explosion that demolished a Nazi tank.

## Gold

Sheffield Park has been many places over the decades, and the film *Gold* took on one of its more exotic roles as Amritsar Junction. In 1948 India won its first Olympic gold medal as an independent nation, for hockey. The winning team's centre forward, Balbir Singh, is widely regarded as one of the best hockey players of all time, and his part in the 1948 victory was the central theme of the Bollywood extravaganza. Bollywood superstar and hearthrob Akshay Kumar took the starring role, and spent the night of filming orbited by devoted acolytes, fetching whatever he wanted and fanning away flies. At Amritsar Junction, the train from Lahore is stopped especially to allow the hockey team to board it.

In the Bollywood tradition, atmosphere is more than accuracy: the Indian train is hauled by Q Class No. 541 with four blood and custard Mk 1s; the engine was disguised by covering the boiler with flour and water to represent limescale and the smokebox with cocoa powder and water to look like rust, and it was fitted with a headlight.

Indian destination boards were added to the carriages, and the platform was crowded with Indian stalls and bustling extras. It was fairly dark anyway, so it all looked fine.

## Christopher Robin

In 2017, two films were made about Christopher Robin, exploring the life of the adult Christopher Milne in different ways. The Disney film *Christopher Robin* concentrated on his life as an adult, and the scenes at the Bluebell depicted him returning the Hundred Acre Wood (in nearby Ashdown Forest), where he is reunited with Winnie the Pooh and friends. Ewan McGregor played Christopher Robin and Hayley Atwell played his wife, Evelyn. Sheffield Park became Hartfield station, where Christopher alights from the train, carrying Pooh. Just as the train is about to depart, Pooh spots a red balloon caught in a carriage door and takes hold of it as they walk away.

Lineside shots were taken of the journey to Sussex, with the scenery through which the train passed very carefully set out with the help of local farmers. Field 1 contained 64 sheep; Field 2 a scarecrow, a woman, and 2 dogs; Field 3 a man and a dog; Field 4 17 cows; and Field 5 3 horses. One hopes that they all remembered to stand in the right place and collected the going rate as extras.

## Goodbye Christopher Robin

This film explores the distant relationship between Christopher Robin and his father, A. A. Milne. The relationship changed completely when the nanny had to go and care for her dying mother, and he was forced to look after his young son himself for a few weeks. They spent the time playing in the woods with Christopher's toys, and so Winnie the Pooh, Piglet, and the others came into being. Spiralling fame, even in the days before social media, quickly got out of hand. Young Christopher was robbed of much of his childhood innocence, and he ended up bullied at boarding school and taunted in the army.

Horsted Keynes became Hartfield station as the young man Christopher Milne left to go to war, seen off by his father. The waiting room was the scene of their final painful interview, when Christopher refuses the vast fortune offered to him by his father, who tries to convince him that the Christopher Robin books would never have been written without the boy himself, so the money was morally just as much his. He boards the train and is carried away, his father with much left to say that never gets said. Milne replays the scene in the waiting room in his head when his son is reported 'missing believed dead', although he does eventually return alive.

## Lyrebird

Once again, a tunnel was the setting for a few days filming, when Sharpthorne Tunnel had another moment of glory, revealing the story of hidden art treasures during the Second World War. Dutch artist Han van Meegeren became infamous, then famous, for forging Vermeer masterpieces and selling them to the Nazis for extortionate prices, claiming them to be originals. After the war he was arrested as a Nazi collaborator, then the paintings were proven to be fakes, and a swift volte-face turned him into a national hero for having swindled the Nazis out of millions. The art world was less forgiving, and considered it to be the art scandal of the century.

When the war started to go badly (from the point of view of the Nazis), they hid what they thought to be their valuable art treasures in a rake of railway wagons in a salt mine near Amsterdam. They were eventually found there after the hostilities by Allied soldiers, who broke into the vans and found the 'Vermeers'.

The salt mine was played by Sharpthorne Tunnel during one long night of filming in April, with the strict proviso that the set had to be struck by 10 a.m. the following morning, before the first train was due. Three vans were painted with Nazi insignia using removable paint (and for once it did what it said on the tin) and the Allied soldiers entered the salt mine to discover them and break them open.

Goods vans were painted with Nazi insignia (using removable paint) for *Lyrebird*.

## Howards End

The novels of E. M. Forster appeared, on the surface, to conjure up an idyllic pre-war Edwardian England of country houses, cricket on the green, young men up at Oxford, and ladies with parasols in long, lazy summers. Beneath it all, however, almost imperceptibly, runs an undercurrent of social repression and the restrictive restraints of class, gender, and money.

In the early 1990s, Merchant Ivory made a series of films based on these stories, and managed perfectly to set the unpalatable themes among beautifully shot sets and locations. These included, on many occasions, Horsted Keynes station and the Bluebell Railway. These included *A Room with a View*, *Where Angels Fear to Tread*, and *Maurice*. At the time, *Howards End* was also made, but none of it filmed at the Bluebell. This oversight was rectified in March 2017 when a film crew came to Sheffield Park to make a four-part adaptation of the book.

Matthew MacFadyen plays Henry in a steamy King's Cross station in *Howards End*, filmed inside the carriage shed at Sheffield Park.

Wealthy and well-connected Mrs Wilcox befriends a younger woman, Margaret Schlegel, and, on an impulse, bequeaths her lovely old country house, Howards End, to Margaret. Upon her death, her husband Henry chooses to suppress the will, producing an earlier version instead, although he eventually marries Margaret and she moves in to Howards End with him. Meanwhile, Margaret's younger sister Helen becomes involved with a bank clerk called Leonard Bast, from a lower social order altogether.

The railway scenes were filmed inside the carriage shed at Sheffield Park, which was transformed into King's Cross in 1905. The platform was built over B Road with a train on either side, the Mets on one side with the C Class and the Victorian set on the other, and fifty extras to make it look busy. Sheffield Park station became Hilton Park, with the forecourt transformed with new fencing, gravel, and flower beds.

Actor Joe Bannister (Charles Wilcox) drives a 1904 Humber down the drive, and, being unfamiliar with the car, is instructed to aim between two white posts and mind the camera – a shot that was filmed only once! C Class No. 592 and the Victorian carriages were also filmed between Sheffield Park and Horsted Keynes, the C Class thinly disguised with 'London and Northern' logos on the tender.

Tracey Ullman, who played Aunt Juley, recalled making her music video for 'Move Over Darling' with *Stepney* at Sheffield Park in 1983 (although she was somewhat taken aback to be reminded that it was that long ago) and read the write-up about it in the first edition of this book. The story and photos brought back happy memories, and she agreed to pose at the same place on the platform where she had danced alongside *Stepney* in the video.


## *Summerland*

In October 2018 Horsted Keynes station and cottages featured in a film set in 1941. The film focuses on the life of the fiercely independent writer Alice (Gemma Arterton), obliged to take in an evacuee much against her wishes. Haunted by a past lover and consumed by her work, she finds that her outlook on life gradually changes after she takes in Frank, and her initial resolve to get shot of him as soon as possible begins to weaken.

Several scenes were shot at Horsted Keynes from various points in the story during one long and very busy day. In an early scene at the station, Alice sees the evacuees being doled out by the woman in charge, Mrs Lawrence (Amanda Root), and notices that one small and very forlorn boy stands alone, apart from the others. The station becomes Waterloo later in the day, after Frank has run away from Alice, and, she assumes, taken the train back to London. She was filmed aboard the stationary train, rushing through the carriages and pushing people aside in her frantic search for the boy.

While walking up from the station, to film some scenes on the bridge, the film crew passed the cottages and admired them, and my husband Mick mentioned that we lived in one of them. The director then decided to use our garden in one scene, where Frank and his friend Edie, a fellow evacuee, are collecting scrap metal for the war effort. They were trundling along a homemade soapbox cart, and Frank spots a rusty shovel in the front garden and goes in to collect it, Mick having first shut the dogs round the back and moved the picnic table. The only other incongruous thing in the garden was the 1950s petrol pump, rescued from the village garage, that we happen to have in the porch. That wasn't easy to move, so it remained 'out of shot'. Our son Henry, when told about this little scene, commented that Frank should have gone round the back to the shed, where he would have found enough scrap metal for a couple of Spitfires.

During the years of the Covid pandemic and the long, drawn-out period of 'coming out of lockdown', a few films were still made and set on the Bluebell, all working under the restrictions imposed at the time and coping with Covid testing, social distancing, and mask wearing.

## Mothering Sunday

In October 2020, this film was based on the novel by Graham Swift and set in Beechwood in England on a special day, Sunday 30 March 1924. Mothering Sunday falls on the middle Sunday in Lent, and in the early Church it was a day to celebrate the Mother Church and a day of feasting to break up the long forty-day Lenten fast. Only in the last century or so has it had anything to do with motherhood, a tradition gradually evolving from the day that girls in service were allowed off to go home and visit their own mothers.

Maid Jane Fairchild (Odessa Young) is in service in the Niven household and has gone off, as all the maids do, to go and visit their mothers. However, she was orphaned at birth and has no mother, so she uses the opportunity to spend the day with her lover Paul, the son of a wealthy family. At Sheffield Park, which became Titherton station, all the maids of the household, dressed in their Sunday best and carrying posies for their mothers, are lined up along the platform, awaiting their train. All seemed to be going well, and the first take was a promising one ... except that two of the maids were still wearing their masks.

Sheffield Park booking hall and waiting room were painstakingly transformed into the interior of an Oxford tea shop. This took two days of set dressing to achieve, but on the day the unit ran out of time and the set was never used. Many of the unused props were discarded – we ended up the richer by four candles.

## Living

Mr Williams (Bill Nighy) is a veteran civil servant in 1950s London who becomes a cog in the bureaucracy of rebuilding post-war England. The job, unsurprisingly, becomes all-consuming, and during this time he learns that he only has seven months to live. The realisation concentrates his mind and he embarks on a quest to find some meaning in what remains of his life and do what we would now call 'ticking things off a bucket list', indulging in a spree along the South Coast.

Sheffield Park station platforms and the interior of the carriage shed were used to depict scenes from Mr Williams' life before he veered from the straight and narrow. Sheffield Park became Walton-on-Thames, the platform crowded with commuters as the train arrives, its progress followed by a drone from the station and along the line.

The interior of the carriage shed became Esher station, where the commuters boarded and the train left the station without any form of traction being involved. The carriage remained stationary, and a moving platform was built alongside it. The commuters on the platform were pushed past the carriage window to create the illusion, from the camera position inside, that the train was moving. Not quite as daft as it sounds; every engine driver is familiar with the moment when an adjacent train pulls away, prompting that instinctive lunge for the vacuum brake!

## The 2020s

During this decade, there has been a move away from film companies always requiring platforms, stations, engines, and rolling stock. The carriage sheds at Sheffield Park and Horsted Keynes have been used as film studios, with sets and special effects providing the railway scenes.

The period of lockdown, inevitably, caused a bit of a hiatus in the filming calendar, but the railway and the film industry were adaptable, and it wasn't long before the cameras were back rolling again, working within the restrictions that became so familiar for a while. 'Back to normal', at one time, seemed to be ever moving forward into an uncertain future, but it came, and the film units returned.

# Postscript

In the last half a century, the way that films are made and the means that we have for viewing them have changed immeasurably and in ways that could never have been predicted. If we could step back onto the platform at Sheffield Park on that day in 1960 when *The Innocents* was being filmed and inform the crew that, within their lifetimes, it would be possible to make and view a piece of film using a wireless telephone the size of a playing card – and that everyone would be doing it – we would have been a laughing stock. Such was the stuff of sci-fi.

We have moved from rolls of film made and shown on reels to digital technology and CGI special effects, and from the early days of black and white TV pictures, through video and DVD to Blu-ray and Netflix.

The Bluebell Railway, too, has grown beyond all early expectation in that time, which has had a bearing on the use that the film companies can make of our facilities. In 1960, steam trains were still a common sight on the railway network, although the pioneers of the railway heritage movement who founded the Bluebell could see the writing on the wall for steam, and they had read and understood it.

Once established, heritage railways soon became an interesting phenomenon in themselves, and the Bluebell made many appearances, mainly on local TV. 'Look at these people volunteering to run their own railway – an airline pilot driving the train, a doctor in the signal box and a bus driver laying the track; what fun they're all having!' was generally the tone of the piece. Nowadays, heritage railways are so much a part of the scene that they are no longer considered a novelty in themselves.

Special effects have moved on in leaps and bounds from the days of *The Onedin Line*, when grainy black-and-white archive film of a ship in a storm would be inexpertly cut with someone throwing buckets of water over Captain Baines on his tilting deck; the Bluebell has staged some spectacular train crashes and explosions, and the development of blue-screen backgrounds has placed the Bluebell stations and lineside all over the world.

There were concerns that CGI would become so good that actual trains would not be required, but it appears that nothing really looks as much like a real train as a real train does, and real trains are still in demand. In recent years, camera and lighting equipment has become so much lighter and easier to transport and power that film producers are using locations more, not less, than they used to, which bodes well for railway scenes in the future.

It is a relationship that works well. They want steam trains, we provide them, they pay us, we use the money to preserve steam trains … *Floreat Vapor!*

**A full chronological filmography from six decades and more, several with links to official film trailers, can be found at bluebell-filming.co.uk/filmography.**

# About the Author

Heidi Mowforth was born in 1961 and has been a volunteer at the Bluebell Railway since 1981. She writes regular filming reports for *Bluebell News* and more recently *Stepney* story books for children. She is a steam locomotive driver, and has been a volunteer in the locomotive department since 1981.

Her love of steam and heritage railways extends beyond the Bluebell, and she is a regular driver on the Kent & East Sussex Railway and North Norfolk Railway, and was a North Yorkshire Moors Railway fireman for twenty years. She and her husband own and rally miniature traction engines and also volunteer on a miniature railway at Pulborough, West Sussex.

In between stints on the iron road, she serves at the altar at St Giles' Church in Horsted Keynes and works as a classroom assistant in the village school. She is married to Mick Blackburn, who has been a Bluebell volunteer since the railway was founded. They live in a former railway cottage at Horsted Keynes station, and have two adult children and two grandchildren.

Heidi was the first woman in Britain to have driven more than 140 different steam locomotives, which she regards as her life's greatest achievement and privilege.